Abraham H. Maslow: A Memorial Volume

International Study Project, Inc.
Menlo Park, California

Compiled with the Assistance of
Bertha G. Maslow

Brooks/Cole Publishing Company
Monterey, California

A Division of Wadsworth Publishing Company, Inc.
Belmont, California

ISBN: 0–8185–0033–6
L.C. Catalog Card No: 74–178890
Printed in the United States of America
1 2 3 4 5 6 7 8 9 10—76 75 74 73 72

This book was edited by Micky Stay and designed by Linda Marcetti. It was typeset, printed, and bound by Kingsport Press, Inc., Kingsport, Tennessee.

Foreword

This memorial to my husband affords the opportunity to make public the tributes, recollections, and feelings expressed by some of his friends and colleagues upon his death. Also, it provides the vehicle for sharing Abe with these friends and colleagues. I have selected some of his writings on various topics—some notes and scribblings that reflect a bit of his thinking, his insights, his frustrations, and his wit. I hope that by reading through the volume, you will get a sense of the more private, personal aspects of Abe.

Although no attempt was made to structure these diverse bits and pieces, a rather loose organization did appear during the development of the volume. The first section contains the reflections, thoughts, and eulogies made by some of Abe's colleagues at the time of his death. The second section grew out of Abe's last public seminar, held in March 1970 at the University of California, Los Angeles. The seminar session was captured on tape and expertly edited by Robert Tannenbaum. The third section contains excerpts from previously unpublished material of Abe's. I chose these pieces to emphasize areas in which Abe was especially misread, misinterpreted, or misunderstood. And by the stark, excerpted nature of the selections, I hope to have intensified the message. I have tried to include dates for the excerpted material whenever possible. The final section is a complete chronological bibliography, which should prove helpful for further research or study or to those interested in reading some of Abe's other writings.

The desire to express gratitude overcomes my natural inclination to be cool. The situation calls for a rhapsodic treatment. Abe and I had the unparalleled good fortune to be associated with the W. P. Laughlin Charitable Foundation,* and especially with William P. Laughlin and William J. Crockett. These men and the other members of the Board, James W. Morrell and Sherman A. Moore, as well as their wives, Jayne Laughlin, Verla Crockett, Marylyn Morrell, and Alice Moore, have been particularly interested and supportive. Others at Saga Administrative Corporation also offered the climate and conditions absolutely ideal for Abe's work. He was ecstatically happy and productive during his too-short tenure as a Fellow with the Foundation.

Needless to say, I deeply appreciate the unusual quality and the degree of cooperation of those who contributed to this memorial volume, especially Robert Tannenbaum, who so unselfishly gave of his thinking and writing, which initiated this entire project. Also, I thank Katherine A. Pontius, Joseph S. Shakes, and William L. Warner for their support and guidance during some difficult times, and William H. Hicks, editor with Brooks/Cole Publishing Company, who extended himself over and above the line of duty.

Bertha G. Maslow

* The W. P. Laughlin Charitable Foundation has been renamed International Study Project, Inc., and has responsibility for coordinating publication of additional writings of Abraham H. Maslow.

Contents

Part One

&❧

Memorial Service Honoring Abraham H. Maslow, Brandeis University, October 25, 1970

&❧

(Rabbi Albert S. Axelrad):*

Ladies and gentlemen, I welcome you to the Berlin Chapel. We are gathered here this morning to do honor to the life and to the memory of Abraham Maslow—a dear friend, a teacher, and a colleague. Our service this morning will be a simple service at which several of Dr. Maslow's friends, colleagues, teachers, and students will speak. We call upon a friend of Abraham Maslow's, Professor Frank Manuel.

* Brandeis University

3

(Professor Frank Manuel): *

There are some of us who live with the weight of the historical experience of mankind upon our shoulders. We are obsessed with the past to a degree that action is obliterated—and sometimes even hope. Others among us are so intoxicated with the presence of present time that, like fireflies, we are oblivious to anything else. And then there are those who, though far from any traditional religious expectation of ultimate redemption, live in the constant presence of the future. These secular futurists construct an ideal world for themselves and populate it with images that are illusions to the historian and the realist. But theirs remains a compelling and enduring way of experiencing life. Abraham Maslow was a builder of psychological utopias which he inhabited always. And from time to time he invited his friends and readers throughout the world to visit with him. He was a great inventor of neologisms to describe these fantasies—his favorite was eupsychia. And even the most skeptical among us, who sometimes would mock him tenderly as he unfolded his ideas, would return from a sojourn to his eupsychia marvelously refreshed, much like waking from a pleasant dream. The civilized world has never been without utopias. Almost every society brings forth men whose appointed mission it seems to be to dream of otherness for us less imaginative fellows immersed in our daily tasks. Utopians like Abe Maslow have been possessed by a vision of the potential grandeur and vitality of man. We could not live without these men of fantasy—any more than an individual creature can long survive without his daily portion of sleep and dreaming. When utopia dies, the society is spent.

But Maslow was also a man of science, whose curiosity ranged further than almost any investigator's I have known. From his early boyhood he was forever poking his nose into every aspect of human behavior. He was open to every hypothesis, however outlandish it might appear to the established school. All were welcome. All—that is—except one powerful band of contemporaries whom he fought throughout his life: those committed to the false

* Kenan Professor of History, New York University

4

idol of the neutrality and indifference of positivistic science, those glorifying their mechanical and mathematical tools as if they were gods. I remember how disturbed Abe was when the American Psychological Association elected him president and he attended his first board meeting with the potentates of that academic Leviathan. What had he done, he kept asking morosely, what had become of him, when it was possible for those positivistic piddlers to choose him. He must have taken a wrong turn—betrayed his ideal in some respect—if they could select him. I sat consoling him one afternoon, assuring him that they were only trying to seize the instruments of utopia, that the power elite always operated in that fashion, and that he would be untouched by them. And so he was.

With Walter Grether in monkey lab at
University of Wisconsin, 1935

In a sense, Abe harked back to a seventeenth-century view that regarded science as a synthetic whole in the service of man. The ideal of pansophia, of a unitary science, which Bacon and Comenius and Leibniz dreamed of in the youth of the scientific age, was still his. But Maslow called it humanist and, as a good Jewish anticlerical who came to maturity in the 1930s, he would never have accepted their religious framework. The seventeenth-century

High school graduation, 1926

6

pansophians taught that knowledge that did not lead to God would lead to the devil. Abe in his secular version of the same thought believed that knowledge purporting to be value-free, Galilean, objective, could lead to destruction. The mere accumulation of facts and the fragmentation of science into a thousand discrete elements outraged him, as did the tendency of quantification techniques to give status to that knowledge, however trivial. We all remember—at least many of his friends do, I am sure—his saying: "If something is not worth doing, it is not worth doing well."

In recent years Abe Maslow's day had come; the establishment had at last caught up with the forethinker. Abe had been a sexologist in an American university at a time when the name of Freud was not often mentioned in the classroom. Abe worked with primates long before the current obsession with the ethological analogy. Abe studied the Blackfoot Indians long before it became common to psychologize anthropology. For him there was one science of man. When he arrived at this university [Brandeis], the literary people among us rejoiced at the presence of a humanist psychologist, to open the new field that then seemed dominated by behaviorists.

Abe Maslow had an unquenchable curiosity and seemed to live in a perpetual state of wonderment. I recall his wide-eyed surprise at new things, and especially his warm chuckle over novelty discovered, a sort of assurance that if things were lawful they were on occasion ridiculously so. The historical world was alien to his training, and he would be amazed to find that he was sometimes rediscovering pristine wisdom. And *I* was always amazed at the freshness with which he re-created an ancient idea. It was familiar, and yet there was something new about it: it was Abe's.

But I would not want to leave the impression that this utopia-maker committed to his vision was a babe in the woods. He also had a childlike astuteness that astonished those of us who fancied ourselves knowers of the hard realities of war and bureaucracy and the murderous play of power. It is not without a certain retrospective delight that I now think back to a prehistoric age at Brandeis when what were called the social sciences operated as a unitary body in constant disharmony. We worldly *politiques* in government, sociology, and history discovered one day to our surprise that somehow, accidentally, there were more psychologists

At A. Kardiner's summer home, Westport, Connecticut, 1937

in the social sciences than staff members in all the other fields put together. For who could refuse Abe what he felt was necessary for the furtherance of knowledge?

Abe *liked* to be called a utopian, because for him the word had positive, not negative, connotations. He was utopian not only in his way of thinking, but in his central preoccupation with psychological needs and the attempt to define them. We may or may not agree with Abe's theory of the hierarchy of needs. But that basic matter of the distinction between authentic and inauthentic human needs—one of the major moral problems of Western utopian thinkers—was for him, as it remains for us, a primary question, growing more rather than less acute as our technological civilization becomes more complex. His views on human need could often be encapsulated in a common-sensical anecdote—like the one he used to tell about the quarreling couple: the wife complained to her husband that he was always wanting what he had not got, to which the husband finally responded in exasperation, "And what is there to want but what one has not got?"

Like the more incisive of the utopians, Abe had a sense of humor about his own fantasies and an underlying sadness about the human condition. He dreamed of a grand, heroic world where all men would be strong, fulfilled, and self-actualized; where peak emotional experiences breaking the calm felicity of life would give tonus to the whole of existence; where power would be as irrelevant to all men as it was to him. But those who knew the private as well as the public man soon learned that, like all men of will and of an idea, he was also a great sufferer and was possessed by doubts about himself and his system. My saying this would not have appeared to him either a betrayal of confidence or a contradiction, because Abe was a great truthsayer. Thomas More concluded his *Utopia* with the words: "But I readily admit that there are very many features in the Utopian commonwealth which it is easier for me to wish for in our countries than to have any hope of seeing realized." I believe that Abe on more than one occasion had the same feeling about his own vision of eupsychia.

ஓ

*(Dr. James Klee):**

For psychology the work of A. H. Maslow is one of the great bodies of accomplishment in the twentieth century. His influence permeated, but far outreached, academic psychology. His ideas are now major factors in education, business management, community planning, political theory, religious thought, sociology,

* Associate Professor of Psychology, Brandeis University (on leave) and Professor of Psychology, West Georgia College, Carrollton, Georgia

and medicine. But not only was his work and vision great; most of those who knew him felt that he himself was great. His enthusiasm for a more positive formulation of human life was essentially infectious—eupsychian, as he put it. But more importantly he embodied his own ideals. Never did one feel it was put on. Never was one put down. He truly flowed along so that the action was greater at the crest of this self-generating wave. No matter how badly things went, his lively warmth made one feel it was just a little better close to him.

Both Abe Maslow and William James were giants of the psychological world. Both were occasionally frail, and when they turned a major corner of their lives both suffered physically. Both were identified as suffering heart disease. Both changed not only their minds but their hearts as well—a far more difficult thing to do.

New York City, November 1935

Brooklyn College, 1943

Perhaps that is just a pun. But Aristotle would not have thought so, for in his view the heart was the center for a common sense, integration at its best. James survived his next seizures and ultimately abandoned psychology as a "dirty little science." Abe started to, after his next attack. (Or was the attack part of the process?) He left Brandeis for a more comprehensive post in California, a position in which he could integrate all his work, a refuge from overenthusiastic undergraduate students who resented his lack of formulas for how to actualize their peak experiences and from fearful overspecialized colleagues. He went a changed man—one I felt more wholesome, more adventurous, than ever. He felt after his near-fatal attack in 1967 that anything else was "gravy," as he put it. One sensed a disappearance of the overcautious dietary reserve and concern for health that had characterized so much of his earlier life. Tragically it came too late.

I was tempted to say at first that, like William James, they do not make men like Abe Maslow any more. Now I feel that is not true. Abe's wholesomeness as a psychologist, like James', if anything, points up the need for more of it. Lewis Mumford has recently made the same observation about Leonardo da Vinci. They were not only historical figures; they were the living proof that wholesomeness is not only possible but, as we recognize it, a necessity and, the longer we delay it, a neurosis-producing deficiency. Abe used to mock his colleagues' concern with research exactitude: "Whatever was not worth doing was not worth doing well." He dealt with the whole spectrum of psychology as he saw it, a vision that as far as psychology itself was concerned went beyond James in the dynamic area at least. Like James he excluded little. Indeed, his very enthusiasm for all branches of psychology brought so many specialists to Brandeis that the critical mass of specialists as such was soon reached and psychology lost the humanistic perspective he had forged.

As Abe said later in the second and extensively revised edition of *Motivation and Personality:*

Human life will never be understood unless its highest aspirations are taken into account. Growth, self-actualization, the striving toward health, the quest for identity and autonomy, the yearning for excellence (and other ways of phrasing the striving "upward") must now be accepted beyond question as a widespread and perhaps universal human tendency.

And yet there are also other regressive, fearful, self-diminishing tendencies as well, and it is very easy to forget them in our intoxications with "personal growth," especially for inexperienced youngsters. I consider that a necessary prophylactic against such illusions is a thorough knowledge of psychopathology and of depth psychology. We must appreciate that many people choose

12

the worse rather than the better, that growth is often a painful process and may for this reason be shunned, that we are afraid of our own best possibilities in addition to loving them, and that we are all of us profoundly ambivalent about truth, beauty, virtue, loving them and fearing them too.

But Abe, too, was "human." We often played an identity game which asked "Who or what are you? Answer in a single word or phrase." Abe always said, "a psychologist," although in later years usually with great humor, as if he could no longer help it. Yet his vision was of the whole healthy man, not just the eye, or memory, or reflex, or need, or brain, or neurotic wreck.

ॐ
(*Abram L. Sachar*):*

Abe Maslow was an early colleague here, as many of you in this little chapel know. We were striving hard for a foothold in the academic world. When he came, our faculty numbered thirty-six. We were, as yet, an unaccredited school; we had to wait until we had graduated a number of classes before we could qualify for accreditation. Abe already had a distinguished record. He was much sought after. He could have chosen almost at will where to go, and after he was here he had innumerable calls to other institutions of learning. He preferred to stay here because he shared in the concept that had brought it into being. He was a valuable colleague in planning; he collaborated with a dozen or more of our senior people in guiding the future of the school.

Two principles, I believe, were always paramount as he headed the first Psychology Department. The first was the necessity for diversification in schools of thought. He wanted the clash of ideas within his department. He would have been outraged to watch the growth of cells in which only those would be admitted who subscribed to particular lines of thought and action. He chose his faculty on the basis of competence, not on their political views or their economic outlook.

* Chancellor, Brandeis University

13

The second guideline had to do with his judgment on scholarship itself. He always judged the work of a scholar with respect. His evaluation was quite critical, but it was wholesome and it was humane. If he disagreed, he attacked the scholarship but not the scholar. Some of the younger men soon learned that they gained no prestige by substituting invective for judgment. Frank Manuel put it very well when he recalled arguments that he had had with Abe Maslow and how he often disagreed with him. He said Abe disagreed with tenderness. The judgment was perhaps often more telling because it came in this way and not with shrillness and abuse.

I can still hear that voice; it was always calm (he rarely raised it). It was accompanied by an endearing smile. When Abe would not accept a paper, he would suggest to the student "Surely you can do this better!" Abe had the Talmudic approach, where the rebuke is counted as "the chastisement of love."

We here at Brandeis cherish the memory of Abe Maslow as one of the pioneers who helped to lay the foundations of the university. I cherish his memory as a friend because he belonged in the fellowship of the compassionate.

ॐ

(*G. F. Nameche*):*

Our relationship was personal and intellectual at the same time. This was partly because we lived only two blocks from each other in Newton and partly because we were both on to the same subject matter, the same problems, and the same interests at that point in time. It's very hard to make clear what I mean about Abe as a "Hasid." What I mean is that Abe was not teaching only academic, intellectual psychology. What he was teaching was in one sense very personal and in another sense totally impersonal. He was concerned with a vision of human life which had tried to come into history at many points in time. And this vision was at times living Abe totally and profoundly. Abe was the most generous and kind teacher that I had personally ever met in my life. Even when he was failing me in an exam in psychology, it was the kindest failing

* Former graduate student at Brandeis University

14

I had ever experienced. He said to me (and this made all the difference in the world), "Gene, you can do better than that." Next time I did better than that. . . .

§⦿

(Rabbi Axelrad):

Little has been said about Abe Maslow as a Jew, apart from the fact that he considered himself one, and a humanistic one. I remember well several conversations that we had, in all of which emerged—quite strongly and quite obviously—that he was a Jew, in his own mind and in his own heart. I remember well in 1967, at the outbreak of the Six Day War, his anxiety and his concern about the survival of Israel when it was, as they say, "up for grabs," and his generosity at that time as well.

He in fact once commented on that for me, and I think it's something that might be wise for some of us to explore. For in his own heart of hearts, humanism and Judaism were not necessarily mutually exclusive.

§⦿

EULOGY
Delivered by Warren Bennis* at the Stanford Memorial Chapel, Palo Alto, California, for Abraham H. Maslow June 10, 1970

Abe Maslow requires no eulogy, explanation, or interpretation. He is an open book, knowledgeable by his words and his treasured person.

* State University of New York at Buffalo. Now President, the University of Cincinnati.

The first sentence in one of Abe's most important books, *Toward a Psychology of Being*, published in 1962:

There is now emerging over the horizon a new conception of human sickness and of human health, a psychology that I find so thrilling and so full of wonderful possibilities that I yield to the temptation to present it publicly even before it is checked and confirmed and before it can be called reliable scientific knowledge.

It is all there in that one sentence—a sentence that has sentenced psychology to a new life, that has turned it inside-out, or more precisely outside-in: *to gain* truth through personal experience, to be a "courageous knower," to view science (in his own words) "as the only way we have of shoving truth down the reluctant throat."

Science to Abe was life and love—his poetry—and debureaucratizing it (or, as he would prefer, resacralizing it) was his goal. And he was a *conquistador*—a lonely one at that for many years —always advancing with courage and charm like the most seductive crusader.

He wrote in his last book, *The Psychology of Science:*

The assault troops of science are certainly more necessary to science than its military policemen. This is so even though they are apt to get much dirtier and to suffer higher casualties. But somebody has to be the first one through the mine fields.

Science was his poetry, his religion, his wonder. He wrote, also in his *Psychology of Science:*

Science can be the religion of the non-religious, the poetry of the non-poet, the art of the man who cannot paint, the humor of the serious man, and the love-making of the inhibited and shy man. Not only does science begin in wonder, it also ends in wonder.

Then he quotes, approvingly and lovingly, in that same book, a poem by another famous Brooklyn boy, Walt Whitman.

16

Their lives have been co-fated, and the poem should be dedicated:
For Abe.

Whitman writes:

When I heard the learned astronomer,
When the proofs, the figures were ranged in
    columns before me,
When I was shown the charts and diagrams, to add,
    divide, and measure them,
When I sitting heard the astronomer where he lectured
    with much applause in the lecture room,
How soon unaccountable I became tired and sick,
Till rising and gliding out I wandered off by myself,
In the mystical moist night-air, and from time-to-time
Looked up in perfect silence at the stars.

• • •

I quote lavishly from Abe's own work, because his work is his life, and to know one is to greet the other.

I first got to know Abe—or encounter him (like many of us)—through one of his books. It was my senior year at Antioch, and while taking a tutorial with the then-president, Douglas Mc-Gregor, he recommended a book on abnormal psychology written by Abe Maslow and Dr. Mittelmann. It was the first breath of clean writing and fresh air that I had had in all of the courses I had taken up to that time in psychology. It was a book that really drew me into psychology as a calling. I'll never forget in this book, in the frontispiece, there were two panel pictures: one that showed a group of happy-looking gurgling babies in the maternity room of a children's hospital—newborn babies—and just beneath that was another panel showing a group of people—haggard, drawn, and sallow—crowded into the New York subway hanging on, with the most baleful looks, to the straps above their heads, and through the windows you could see these sallow faces of the adults. And the caption beneath these two panels was "What happened?" And that's the question that Abe spent most of his life trying to answer.

That was my first encounter with Abe, and my last was in Buffalo in the spring of 1968, when he was on his way to Columbus, Ohio, to visit his new granddaughter and celebrate her birth.

17

Winter 1942

And at that time I conducted a long interview with Abe Maslow from which we made a film. He said to me at that time in Buffalo, right after the filming of our interview, "I have to make an important decision." He knew at that time that to write at all took all the energy he could still muster. He said: "Have I written all the good psychology I can expect to write?" It was brought to a head by Bill Laughlin's marvelous offer to join him in California. He said: "I hesitated for days and then, with Bertha's approval, I refused all the other offers from the major universities to go out West and to spend my full time writing." He said, "I am about to cut myself adrift from all external circumstances—no Harvards, no Brandeises. I want to make a last song, sweet and exultant."

18

In between the first encounter with Maslow and Mittelmann at Antioch and the visit to Buffalo were crowded many lovely times with the Maslows, shimmering, genial, and warm visits, always graced by Bertha's effortless sociability (like the meandering Charles River outside the wooden deck in their Newton home) and her crowded and sumptuous refrigerator. And always Abe—with that incredibly soft, shy, tentative, and gentle voice making the most outrageous remarks. Breakfast with the Maslows was intellectual nirvana—good and endless food, good and endless talk—where always I had the distinct feeling of gaining energy, of being lifted off my feet.

Franck, the Nobel Laureate in physics, once said: "I always know when I hear a good idea because of the feeling of terror which seizes me." In this respect, Abe was a terrorist—a terrorist always bursting through the barricades of conventional wisdom and outdistancing emplaced cannon.

I always sensed, when with Abe, a childlike spirit of innocence and wonder—always wearing his eyebrows (as Thomas Mann said about Freud) continually raised in a constant expression of awe. Abe wrote, about Aldous Huxley, what I consider to be actually an accurate self-description of Abe Maslow:

> May I mention one more such technique that I saw at its best in Aldous Huxley, who was certainly a great man—one who was able to accept his talents and use them to the full. He managed it by perpetually marveling at how interesting and fascinating everything was, by wondering like a youngster at how miraculous things are, by saying frequently, "Extraordinary, extraordinary!" He could look out at the world with wide eyes, with unabashed innocence, awe, and fascination—which is a kind of admission of smallness, a form of humility—and then proceed calmly and unafraid on the great tasks he set for himself.

And, of course, during these years Abe was making history by remaking psychology. So many of the terms, phrases, and concepts now accepted, even into the national vernacular, are Abe's: *need hierarchy, self-actualization, peak experiences.*
And all that went into the Third Force of psychology as Humanistic Psychology.

Anthony Sutich said recently: "Abraham Maslow is the greatest psychologist since Freud. The second half of this century belongs to him."

If the first half of this century saw modern psychology take the mind and heart out of psychology, then Abe Maslow, under heroic conditions, disinterred them—more burnished than before. He wrote:

> In exchange for Freud, Adler, Jung, Fromm, and Horney, we are offered beautifully executed, precise, elegant experiments which, in at least half the cases, have nothing to do with enduring human problems and which are written primarily for other members of the guild. It is so reminiscent of the lady at the zoo who asked the keeper at the zoo whether the hippopotamus was male or female. "Madam," he replied, "it would seem to me that that would be of interest only to another hippopotamus."

• • •

For me—perhaps for all humanistic scholars—Abe's core legacy was to revive the full humanness to science by declaring *all* of our human experiences as capable of study. He wrote, in the final pages of his *Toward a Psychology of Being:*

> All the world, all of experience, must be open to study. Nothing, not even the "personal" problems, need to be closed off from human investigation. Otherwise we will force ourselves into the idiotic position that some labor unions have frozen themselves into: where only carpenters may touch only wood. New materials and new methods must then be annoying and even threatening catastrophes rather than opportunities. I remind you also of the primitive tribes who must place everyone in the kinship system. If a newcomer shows up who cannot be placed, there is no way to solve the problem but to kill him.

For Abe—for us—each man's task is to become the best "himself." Joe Doakes must not try to be like Abraham Lincoln or Thomas Jefferson or any other model hero. He must become the best Joe Doakes in the world. This he can do, and only this is necessary or possible. Here he has no competition.

What Abe has done is to make what was religious, mystical, or supernatural *natural*—to give man ownership over his human

20

potentials, rather than have them arrogated by the temporal non-human institutions which, at times, science, business, and the church have been.

He quotes Rainier Maria Rilke, who said: "If your every-day life seems poor to you, do not accuse it; accuse yourself; tell yourself you are not poet enough to summon up its riches since to the creator there is no poverty and no poor or unimportant place."

Two big things which Abe gave to all of us: the art and science of becoming more fully human, and the democratization of the soul. For these we will be forever indebted.

Presidential Address, Association for Humanistic Psychology, Miami Beach, Florida, 1970
Denis O'Donovan*

Abe's sense of destiny was a great inspiration to me because I am a little bit that way myself. He had the notion that I was very shy, and he kept encouraging me to put myself forward. Other than that he was a good psychologist! His sense of destiny was combined with a marvelous sense of humor and the ability to put himself into perspective. I remember I felt very strange when we were discussing his book *The Psychology of Science*, which I thought was very good, and Polyani's book, *Personal Knowledge*, which I thought was superb. I was a little squeamish, like the person in the mouthwash ad. Finally it came out just as it does on television. Abe said "Of course Polyani's book is a better book." And I said "Well, I didn't need to worry about that at all." The last thing I received from Abe Maslow was a reprint of a journal which had on the front cover "Abe Maslow was a boring teacher." The very

* Professor of Psychology, Florida Atlantic University

21

last thing I received from him was that criticism of him by a student.

We tend to forget that Maslow pioneered in some areas which are only now becoming hot. The ladies of the women's liberation movement have been so very much with us today that I should remind them that in 1939, 1940, and 1942 Abe Maslow was doing substantial research and making daring assertions which are very pertinent today. Some of our male psychologists who are worried that if females become liberated they will not be sexy should read Maslow, and the ladies of the liberation movement should read Maslow. Another topic that unfortunately is becoming hot again is authoritarian character structure, which he studied in 1943. . . .

1957

22

Abe was very much at home with strong people. I have known very few people who could relate better with strong people. He was also very much at home with young people. I believe that Maslow's approach and those similar to it offer the most hopeful bridge to bright and rebellious youth. In fact, Maslow himself wrote in great empathy of the young people's dissatisfaction not only with the Establishment but more specifically with orthodox academic psychology. He claimed that the major motivation theories by which man lives lead only to depression or cynicism. I am sure most of you are familiar with his critique of the Freudians in theory (not always in practice) as being deeply reductionistic about our higher human values: "The deepest and most real motivations are seen to be dangerous and nasty while the highest human values and virtues are essentially fake, being not what they seem to be but being camouflaged versions of the deep, dark and dirty." Our social scientists are just as disappointing in the main. "A total cultural determinism," he wrote "is still the official orthodox doctrine of many or most of the social scientists and anthropologists. This doctrine not only denies intrinsic and higher motivations, but comes perilously close sometimes to denying human nature itself."

Another way in which his work of long ago was ahead of most of us is his emphasis on holism. One of the last things that Abe wrote was his tribute to Adler. He said "In one respect especially, the times have not caught up with him. I refer to his holistic emphasis. This is certainly a task for the '70s." This is something that Maslow said of Adler, but we can say it of Maslow: that the implications through research and living of his holism are very suitable tasks for the '70s. . . .

Abe was above all a scientist. He undoubtedly takes some pleasure in being remembered as a good human being, but he wished to be judged as a scientist, and it is as such that I most admire him.

What will be the fate of Maslow's theories? I am afraid that they will not be put to the test. This is an unfortunate prediction, and I don't make it happily. There are many reasons for my being pessimistic about it. The basic reason is that the technology of testing his theories has not been worked out in a way that makes it feasible for young people to build a career out of testing Abe Maslow's ideas. After all, Abe's guiding concept was that, under some circumstances, some people are sometimes capable of magnificence. Now, asking a young person to design a dissertation to come anywhere near testing that concept is calling upon an intrinsic motivation par excellence. In other words, it is the sort of thing one does just for the hell of it rather than to satisfy a committee. . . .

Now, as I said before, Abe Maslow understands the wisdom and benevolence of powerful men. I do not regard in any sense Abe as naïve or mystical. He was a very hard-headed man. . . .

I have an image of Abe Maslow as a person who could not conceive of insides being empty. I have an image of him—as many of you have—as a person who personally experienced, lustily experienced, both the hunger and the satisfaction of the hunger all the way up the hierarchy of his motives from the bottommost to the topmost and experienced them all with gusto. . . .

So now is a suitable time, I think, to look within ourselves to see what is there, which is precisely what he wants us to do. You and you and you and all of us can test Abe Maslow's hypothesis. The most appropriate way to honor a magnificent man is to be magnificent.

In Memoriam to Abraham H. Maslow
Ricardo B. Morant*

Professor Abraham Maslow died on June 8, 1970, at the age of sixty-two at Menlo Park, California. He was at the time on leave of absence from Brandeis to serve as the first Resident Fellow of the W. P. Laughlin Charitable Foundation.** Professor Maslow came to this university in 1951 and became its first chairman of the department of psychology. A founder of what some have called Humanistic Psychology, he won recognition and many honors for

* Fierman Professor of Psychology, Brandeis University
** Now the International Study Project, Inc.

24

his scholarly work. He was a past president of the American Psychological Association.

It is hard to assimilate the thought of Professor Maslow's death. One reason for me personally is that he was my closest friend. We first met eighteen years ago when he asked me to join him here, and over the years we came to know each other well. He was everything that one could want in a colleague and friend. He was straight. There was no cant to him. He felt deeply and believed and acted on what he felt. In the many years of our association, I never once questioned his commitment or loyalty or love. He gave these freely. He gave of his emotions and intellect openly to all of his colleagues and students and friends. We, in the academy, mourn his death but find solace in the recognition that the ideas he so cherished continue to live.

Fall 1957

25

A second reason why it's hard to accept the thought of Professor Maslow's death is that he was so alive. He led a fuller life than most, for he lived with an eye to the future. He was much concerned about the implications of present ideas and actions for future developments and tried to shape them so that they would come out right. His work at the time of his death, for example, was devoted to the analysis of the requirements of a good society. But he was no Cassandra. His task was not to warn or scold or create fears of the future. Quite the contrary. He believed that things would turn out right if given half a chance. He was a humanist who fervently believed in the worth of human existence. He believed in life. He was not of those who see life as an existential conundrum to be despised because there are no first principles.

There was a first principle for Maslow, and that was that man's basic nature is good. He wasn't naïve about this; he didn't think that virtue and truth would always prevail against the odds. Nothing like that. It was more as if he thought that there was some slight cosmological leaning—some quirk in nature—which had biased the laws of chance to favor the development of man and man's goodness. But he felt that the bias toward goodness was slight and could be overwhelmed. It was, as he called it, instinctoid in man rather than instinctive: not powerful, not overpowering, but nevertheless there for us to discover and nourish.

And this was his self-imposed task as a psychologist: to find that germ of goodness, describe it, and show us how it should be developed. This task in retrospect is already implicit in his earliest work. His studies in the thirties and forties on motivation, the hierarchy of needs, the analysis of dominance and security feelings, the relationship between self-esteem and sexuality—all these early studies we can see now lead directly to his later work on the self-actualizing person and the problem of psychological health.

Jorge Luis Borges, the Argentinean poet and essayist, reminds us that a great author creates his own precursors—that in the author culminates a series of apparently diverse ideas and influences whose similarity and continuity are defined only in terms of his own work. The same can be said of a great social scientist. He creates those ideas which prefigured him. Maslow published scholarly work in experimental, clinical, personality, counseling, comparative, and industrial psychology, as well as in sociology,

26

anthropology, and the philosophy of science. He was identified as a Freudian but also as a behaviorist and also as an existentialist. He felt ill at ease with these many public identities that his work had given him. For he was no one of these. He was not a philosopher nor an anthropologist nor an industrial psychologist nor a clinician; nor did he belong to any one school of psychology. He was rather what each of these disciplines and schools had in common as defined in him. He searched in his later years for a name that would better circumscribe his unique view of the study of human nature. He coined or accepted different names to define that trend in the history of ideas which he, in Borges' sense, had created. He was not satisfied for long with any of the names—existential psychology, humanistic psychology, third force psychology, the psychology of self-actualization, the psychology of being—or with the definition of the trend which he had set. His death clarifies the outline of the trend and simplifies the problem of what to call it. It is already being referred to by many as Maslovian Psychology.

For those who knew Maslow, it is obvious that the name could only have been used after his death. For were he alive, the title of his next book surely would be *Beyond Maslovian Psychology*. And therein lies both the tragedy and greatness of this man. He founded no schools during his lifetime, for he always went beyond his students and disciples. He never stopped to exhaustively explore a small area, for his goal, as he saw it, could only be reached by approximations, by large tacks requiring great changes in direction. We can now see that the apparent changes always led forward to his goal. His death will create the school which could not be created during his life, for Maslow will not be here to deny it—to go beyond it. The real tragedy is that his death deprives us of the real Maslovian Psychology. It deprives us of knowing those precursors of his own thinking which this fertile mind would have continued to create.

Maslow and I argued frequently about his optimism. Where I and others could see only change, he saw development, growth—directional change which gave him hope. One is reminded of the story of the cosmological constant introduced to reconcile the astronomical data with Einstein's concept of a relativistic universe. Einstein, in the face of the facts, rejected the constant which he had himself introduced; his view of the universe was too clear to be muddled by such data. Better observations (decades later, of course) proved what he had known right along. Like Einstein, Maslow also sensed a different cadence than most of us. For our own sake, we can only pray that he also sensed more clearly.

Let me add just one more thing, and now I address myself only to those of you who knew Abe intimately and have wondered how he felt during this past year away from his friends and after his heart attack. Bertha assures me that he was happier than he had ever been. The following is from a tape which he sent to the editors of *Psychology Today* just before his death. Abe, who had just finished a major piece of work, reminisced about an earlier heart attack which had come after he had finished something he was pleased with. These are Abe's words:

Menlo Park, California, April 1970 (photo courtesy of William Carter)

I had really spent myself. This was the best I could do, and here was not only a good time to die but I was even willing to die. . . . It was what David M. Levy called the "completion of the act." It was like a good ending, a good close. I think actors and dramatists have that sense of the right moment for a good ending, with a phenomenological sense of good completion—that there was nothing more you could add. . . . Partly this was entirely personal and internal and just a matter of feeling good about myself, feeling proud of myself, feeling pleased with myself, self-respecting, self-loving, self-admiring. . . .

My attitude toward life changed. The word I use for it now is the post mortem life. I could just as easily have died, so that my living constitutes a kind of an extra, a bonus. It's all gravy. Therefore I might just as well live as if I had already died.

One very important aspect of the post mortem life is that everything gets doubly precious, gets piercingly important. You get stabbed by things, by flowers and by babies and by beautiful things—just the very act of living, of walking and breathing and eating and having friends and chatting. Everything seems to look more beautiful rather than less, and one gets the much-intensified sense of miracles.

I guess you could say that post mortem life permits a kind of spontaneity that's greater than anything else could make possible.

If you're reconciled with death or even if you are pretty well assured that you will have a good death, a dignified one, then every single moment of every single day is transformed because the pervasive undercurrent—the fear of death—is removed. . . . I am living an end-life where everything ought to be an end in itself, where I shouldn't waste any time preparing for the future or occupying myself with means to later ends. . . .

Sometimes I get the feeling of my writing being a communication to my great-great-grandchildren, who, of course, are not yet born. It's a kind of an expression of love for them, leaving them not money but in effect affectionate notes, bits of counsel, lessons I have learned that might help them. . . .*

His message ends at this point.

* Reprinted from *Psychology Today* Magazine, August, 1970. Copyright © Communications/Research/Machines, Inc.

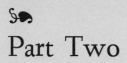

Part Two

Robert Tannenbaum,
University of California,
Los Angeles, July 1970[*]

Following are some personal observations with respect to Abe. They have been affected very much by discussions I have had with my wife, Edith, about her feelings toward Abe, too. I will present these observations in separate paragraphs rather than try to develop a fully connected theme around Abe.

There were many childlike qualities about Abe. He often approached ideas and new experiences with the freshness and wonderment of a child in his first confrontation with a new aspect of the world. This childlike quality was also reflected in a naïveté in many matters of everyday living, as well as in a great curiosity about and enthusiasm for all elements of the world around him.

[*] Professor of Behavioral Science, Graduate School of Management, University of California, Los Angeles

Abe was an open person. He was open both to the ideas of others and to experiences. He was quite receptive to new ideas, and he thoroughly enjoyed playing with them in his mind and testing them against his own earlier ideas and experiences. Abe was also open with his own feelings and ideas. And he was often willing to risk with his openness. For example, his notes in *Eupsychian Management* were bound together in a mimeographed book without editing, addition, subtraction, or other change beyond correction of typographical and clerical errors. The notes themselves had been spontaneously dictated every day as a result of his experiences at Non-Linear Systems a few years ago.

Abe had a wonderful facility for listening to people. In doing so, he was able to give them a genuine feeling that he was learning from them—that he had something to really gain from them. Many people experienced this quality of Abe's. He had a habit of carrying blank cards or papers in his pocket; often, as someone was talking with him, Abe would take out the blank paper and jot down notes to ensure that he would remember what was keyed off in him by the other person.

Abe had a facility for conveying to others a deep respect for their ideas and their projects, and he generated in them enthusiasm and high motivation for pursuing these projects. This quality of Abe's was instrumental in motivating such things as the writing of many articles and books by others, the starting of Esalen, the beginnings of the *Journal of Humanistic Psychology* and the *Journal of Transpersonal Psychology*, and many other similar ventures.

Abe was extremely modest—even humble. At times he could hardly believe that he was really the Abe Maslow that other people saw him as being. He was able to assert his own intellectual positions—even when they were unpopular—but he did so with a humility, and he had no need to brag. In relating himself both professionally and personally to others, he did not have a need to overawe. He was also a person who was quite simple in his personal tastes. He did not live ostentatiously.

Abe saw himself as being an ethical man. He reflected his high ethical standards in his behavior. Most people experienced him as being a very decent human being.

Although Abe had a great capacity to be alone (but not

34

lonely), he thoroughly enjoyed interacting with others. He was delighted with people—particularly "good" people.

Abe possessed a strong desire to further the cause of man's humanness. And he used much of his energy in the later years, through writing, speaking, interpersonal dynamics, and so forth, to have as great an impact as he himself could in the furtherance of what he believed in. In his last few years, he was heavily pushed from within to get into print as much as he possibly could. He expressed his concern about the shortness of time still available to him to say what he wanted to say and to have the impact he wanted to.

Abe had a particular talent for developing or extending the use of colorful, mind-catching terms as labels for the ideas he founded: eupsychian, Deficiency and Being, self-actualization, hierarchy of needs, peak experiences (including peakers and non-peakers), and spectator knowledge.

The pages that follow hold special meaning for those who shared Abe's last major public seminar. It was March 17, 1970, the second day of the Organizational Frontiers Seminar at the Graduate School of Management of the University of California, Los Angeles. For almost three hours, Abraham Maslow talked. Freely —without notes—he shared his views, his feelings, and his hopes. His here-and-now presence as the human being that he was deeply moved those of us in the room.

Less than three months later, on June 8, 1970, Abraham Maslow died. Remembering the impact of his contributions that morning, I have attempted to present as fully as possible (but with some minor editing and some rearrangement of his thoughts to bring them together under relevant headings) Abe's insights, wisdom, and humor.

§❧

Hopefulness and Despair

I can see our current situation as part of an unnoticed revolution that's going on. I phrase this in terms of a clash of cultures. On the one hand is the culture of courage and coping and fighting back and striving, which all imply hopefulness of a certain kind, or at least possibility, if not probability. Then, on the other hand, is a culture of despair, of hopelessness, of a theory of evil which has pervaded certain groups in our population.

Photo courtesy of Marcia Roltner

This history of ideas, the history of Western civilization, has been essentially a history of debunking that includes a good 90 percent of the people whom we call great and who have formed us and who are in our blood. We're all Newtonians, we're all Platonists, we're all Freudians, we're all Marxians, we're all Max Weber-types, and so on. I would like you to think for a moment that these were all purveyors of mistrust, suspicions, debunking—having us lose our faith in what we see before our eyes—always feeling that there

36

was something behind what we see and therefore we mustn't trust ourselves. The general thrust of Western history (the history of ideas, I think they are calling it now) has been in terms of blows not to the narcissism of man, but to the trustfulness of man—to trust in human nature, to trust in the possibility of progress, of improvement, and so on. These blows have been made again and again, so that I see ourselves as having been thrust to some extent into a slightly paranoid-like position. You can't trust reasons because they're really rationalizations. You can't trust organizations because the class interests are behind what they are doing.

My own recent work has dealt with what I've been calling "metamotivation"—that is, with the external verities, the intrinsic values, and the role that they play in our motivations. Once we've solved the lower problems, the material problems, empirically I insist on the tremendous role of the metamotivations—the search for truth and excellence and perfection and beauty and justice and ultimate order and ultimate simplicity and harmony and species-hood and brotherhood and the like. The more I get convinced—I speak now with confidence—but I assure you that this means years of conflict and uncertainty and feeling "am I crazy?"

As I meet a very fine man, all the resources that are available to me for understanding that fine man debunk him so that he's seeking either for power or for selfish purposes of some sort or other and so on. I would like you to think that we have been taught by the history of Western civilization that goes back to Plato that what you see isn't really true, but there's something behind it which you have to get at. We have been thrust into a position of despair. If you'd spend as much time thinking about that and trying to figure it out and trying to understand it and trying to feel it as I have during the last few years, I think you would come up finally with the kind of anger which I have toward the carriers of the culture of despair in our society, let alone other societies. Now I'm not talking about skepticism, which I think is quite reasonable and acceptable at this point. But I'm talking about people who are convinced and who will proceed on the assumption that we're all a bunch of bastards, essentially, and that if we behave nicely that this is a fake and there is something behind it and there is something in it for us someplace and that this is all hypocrisy and phoniness.

This is the attitude which I would say is getting through to our college students. Recently I was told by one professor about one of my books (*Toward a Psychology of Being*, which I don't think is especially optimistic) that it is empirical. It's a report of the kind of facts which the culture of despair prefers not to look at, if you don't mind my saying so. She reported to me what this boy had said—that reading this book was for him a different quality of experience. After four years at college he realized now, in his senior year, that every single professor he had had, in every single course that he had had, had convinced him that human nature was evil and not to be trusted. This was, in his senior year, the first book that he had read which had something good to say for people.

I think that something new is happening all through the course of history, and I'm talking now about the history of 2500 years. I think for the first time a synthesis is being offered which is not despairing and which is not based upon the assumption of depravity or of original sin or of essential evil or of essentially teaching you to mistrust your own eyes or of teaching that it's only the nonhuman, nonpersonal things that are really real and that all of the things that are important to us are not really real. Which is like saying that we don't count.

I think that what we are offering now is the possibility for the first time of a positive synthesis, a trust in man, and a trust in society. And I mean to be as Olympian as I possibly can about this. I'm talking about a comprehensive philosophy of life—a philosophy of everything, a philosophy not only of psychology and of human nature and society but of all the professions, of all the social institutions, of the possible future for man. This is now a possibility which is at least at the point where you can write it down. You can talk about the humanistic way of life—this is possible—the humanistic ethos, let's say. And so something new is happening.

If we talk in terms of probabilities, I'd say there is a real probability that we must take into account that the world may be blown up and we with it. This is clearly possible. On the other hand, there is this other possibility of the march of truth, of facts, of science in the new humanistic sense. I would feel the chances are very, very much on the side of this new humanistic synthesis winning out. I don't think that's a foregone conclusion by any chance, because we may get blown up first. But if we can save ourselves from getting blown up—if we can save ourselves from regressing

38

back into the jungle—then I think that I could make a very good case, if I had the time, for the facts, the data, being on the side of the "humanistic ethos," a new image of society which is primitive but is there and can be talked about, of the possibility of the good society. It's clearly a possibility, we know that much anyhow. The new image of man, the new image of society, then in turn generates what I would think would be next most important: the new image of science, which carries along with it all these new definitions of the old words, a new epistemology, a new metaphysics, a new ethic, a new axiology, a new definition of what the word *fact* means, a new definition of truth, which carries along with it by implication, then, a whole new methodology.

Well, I wanted to say that. It's on my mind. There may be a little anger in it; I feel very angry and sometimes bitter and I feel embattled about the organized bastards who are, unfortunately, given so much voice that they essentially have the microphone in our culture. May I refer you to a revised edition of my book called *Motivation and Personality*, which was originally published about fifteen years ago. By good fortune I've had the time given to me to be able to do a good job of the revision, to work at it instead of doing this in stray moments as professors do—really to work at it hard, to rewrite the whole blasted thing, and to support what I've just been saying with at least preliminary data. May I refer you especially to the preface of that book, which is a kind of personal credo. It's a great condensation of a credo of the kind that I've just been making, of the feeling that I have that we need to understand this in the broadest possible way, to think of ourselves as inbetween worlds—a world which is dead and might just as well be killed, much of it, and a world yet to be born. It's in the process of gestation, you might say. And we're in the middle of it, and that certainly is an ambiguous position. We need not only tolerance for ambiguity but we need great courage as well. There is a possibility that we may survive. There is a possibility—a real possibility—that we can make the good society. There is already a pretty well verified fact that we can improve human nature, that we can make men better; we know how to do that. And I think this can give us the courage in the ambiguous situation not only just to tolerate it but, of course, what I would hope is, to get the hell in there and fight because there's much to fight against. There's much to do.

Photo courtesy of Marcia Roltner

🙋 On Normative Zeal and Being a Good Scientist

What follows is a matter of years of struggle within myself. On the one hand is the matter of being very definitely the ethical man—that is, the man trying to improve the world quite specifically so, trying to improve people. Working at the job takes me into fighting, into battling, into politics more in the Aristotelian sense. I love that and I feel that I ought to do it, and there is something within me that tells me that not only I ought to do it but you ought to do it too. Yet how can I put this together with my profound belief that in the advancement of knowledge lies the salvation of man?

There's a kind of not quite Socratic notion to which I would subscribe and which I think I could document fairly well without going as far as Socrates, to say that bad behavior, evil behavior, is impossible to anyone who knows all the facts that are involved. I will say that in the fighting of evil, bad behavior, stupidity, the old sins of greed, selfishness, and so on, I have a very profound trust and faith in what I've been working at for a lifetime; namely, that I can strengthen my ethical concerns by the advancement of knowledge. That is, I can do good—be a good do-gooder—by being a good scientist. Now the only thing is that that requires some change in the definition of science.

I believe that it can be shown that "normative zeal"—that is, to do good, to help mankind, and to better the world—is quite compatible with scientific objectivity and, indeed, even makes conceivable a better science, a more powerful science. I think science has not fulfilled its function because it has arbitrarily shackled itself by outworn metaphysics. We need a science with a far wider jurisdiction than it now has when it tries to be value-neutral and value-free—leaving values to be arbitrarily affirmed. If you don't do it on the basis of facts, what else can you do it on but the basis of sacred books and revelations—that is, by people who don't know what they are talking about? You are leaving values to be decided by nonempirical people, nonfactual people, nonscientists—and on nonfactual grounds.

This is achieved simply by enlarging our conception of objectivity to include not only spectator knowledge but also experiential knowledge. I've used spectator knowledge as a very vivid phrase to describe much of what we describe as knowledge—that is, the kind of knowledge that I would have about white rats, for instance. This is laissez-faire knowledge, uninvolved knowledge, knowledge about, knowledge from the outside essentially. We need to change from this conception of knowledge and add to it— not displace it altogether, but add to it—experiential knowledge, knowledge by participation, the way in which my knowledge of human beings, for instance, is more experiential than my knowledge

41

of geese or white rats, and what I may call (this is really bold; I hope you don't mind) love knowledge—the knowledge which comes from greater perceptiveness, the knowledge about someone, about a person, which comes from the greater perception of loving that person, rather than not caring about him, or not being neutral. And I call this also Taoistic knowledge. The simple model of Taoistic objectivity comes from the phenomenology of disinterested love and admiration for the being of the other person. For instance, loving one's baby, or one's friend, or one's profession, or even one's problem, in the scientific sense, one's field in science, can be so complete and accepting that it becomes noninterfering, nonintrusive— hence the word *Taoistic*.

It is possible to love the truth yet-to-come, to trust it, to be happy, and to marvel as its nature reveals itself. One can believe that the uncontaminated, unmanipulated, unforced, undemanded truth will be more beautiful, more pure, more truly true than that same truth would have been had we forced it to conform to a priori expectations or hopes or plans or current political needs or current intellectual fashions. Truth can also be born into this same invisible strait jacket. "Normative zeal" can be wrongly understood and can distort the truth-to-come by a priori demands. And I am afraid that some scientists do just this, in effect, giving up science for politics. But this is not at all a necessity for this new kind of Taoistic scientist who can love the truth yet-to-be-born enough to assume that it will be for the best and for this reason will let it be, precisely for the sake of his "normative zeal."

I, too, believe this: that the purer the truth, and the less contaminated it is by doctrinaires whose minds are made up in advance, the better it will be for the future of mankind. I trust that the world will be more benefited by the truth of the future than by the political convictions which I hold today. Very firmly I may hold them and yet feel also that I don't know enough and that I don't know as much as I would if I could live fifty years longer. I trust what will be known more than I trust my present knowledge. This is a humanistic, scientific version of "not my will but thine be done." My fears and hopes for mankind, my eagerness to do good, my desire for peace and brotherhood, my "normative zeal"—all these I feel are best served if I remain modestly open to the truth, objective and disinterested in this new Taoistic sense of refusing to prejudge the

42

truth or to tamper with it, as our politicians and scientists are now doing.

§🦫

Love for a Child

You can like a child just as it is, with no impulse to change it or to improve it, in the same way that I can love my little grand-daughter, who is so perfect. This is an experience some among you certainly will know about. It's a kind of benign delirium. You have a healthy little child, healthy little baby, well-mothered, well-fathered—well-grandfathered, also. And it's a kind of miracle. And essentially the best reaction to this situation is, of course (if you have any sense) to just enjoy it. You accept it. You don't start educating and training and teaching and having ambitions for the child and so on and so on—not unless you're a dope. A child who is

Photo courtesy of Marcia Roltner

43

healthy can be so perfect that you cannot conceive of being able to make a better job of it. Now this is in the Taoistic sense accepted, the full accepting. This means, it carries along with it also, the Taoistic sense of nonintrusion, of letting be, of noninterference. It takes great love to be able to leave something alone—to let it be and become, in its own nature and its own style. One can love one's child that purely.

It is possible to love one's baby even before it is born and to wait with bated breath and with great happiness to see what kind of person it will be and now to love that future person. Even as a six-year-old girl can have fantasies about her future babies and how much she loves them. They haven't even been conceived yet. And yet it's possible; this is a possible phenomenon. A priori plans for the child, ambitions for it, prepared roles, even hopes that it might become this or that—all these are non-Taoistic. They represent demands upon the child that it become what the parent has already decided it should become. Such a baby is born into an invisible strait jacket. Now the well-loved child, meaning the well-accepted child, does not have such demands placed upon him.

§◦

On Helping

Helping? Well, I have a label for it (labels are good; they are useful for me). I call it the Bodhisattvic Version (Path). We have no good word in English for *helper*; it carries too many surplus connotations with it. I've used the Eastern conception of the Bodhisattvia and transformed it a little bit for our purposes. Do you know what the word means?

There are two Buddhistic legends. In one the Buddha sat under a tree and had the great revelation; he saw the truth. It's very Socratic. He saw the truth, the truth was revealed to him, and then he ascended to heaven, so to speak, to Nirvana. In another version, the Bodhisattvic Version, the Buddha sat under the tree, had a great illumination, saw the truth, ascended to the gates of heaven, and there, out of compassion for mankind, could not bear to selfishly enter heaven and came back to earth to help—on the assumption that nobody could go to heaven unless we all go to heaven.

44

Photo courtesy of Marcia Roltner

So this is a beautiful legend, and what it means for us, I think, is to recognize that helping in the first place is a very, very hard job and the helper can be a clumsy fool—the helper can be a hurter. Very frequently it would be best to be Taoistic about helping; to keep your damn hands off is frequently the best way to help. To know when to be available and when not is to think of the helper as being available, being the consultant, rather than being the manipulator, controller, interferer, giving orders and telling people what to do, which is our choice and which is very Western. The helper comes. The helper is very frequently just a plain goddamn nuisance—as, for instance, anybody in the ghettos can tell you. Why should it be that the social workers, who want to help, who devote their lives to helping, should be so frequently despised and hated?

I've suggested that the Bodhisattvic kind of helping is a reliance on the self-choice of the person with you the helper being available at the wish of the other, rather than you the helper taking control of the situation and telling people what to do. This implies a kind of humility, also, because in effect what I'm asking here is that the helper become a very perfect person. This is a very hard thing to do—that is, to know when to keep your hands off and

45

when to help and when to be available and so on—especially with our young children, where frequently we do have to interfere.

What is implied, therefore, is that one of the paths to being a helper is to become a better and better person, in the psychotherapeutic sense, in the sense of maturing, evolving, becoming more fully human, and so on. If you want to help other people best, improve yourself. Cure yourself. To the extent that you're neurotic or dominating or authoritarian, you're going to hurt other people when you try to help them. To the extent that you can be democratic, accepting, Taoistic, to that extent you are more likely to help them. But this is a paradox, because one of the paths to becoming a better person is via helping other people. You can't become a better person by being selfish, by being within your own skin. So this paradox has to be resolved; it's kind of like the hen and the egg thing, of simultaneously, if you want to be the better helper, improving yourself and being helpful the best way you can—but doing it in the spirit of humility and of modesty rather than in the spirit of taking control.

Photo courtesy of Marcia Roltner

46

The Wholeness of Truth

In my first biology class in high school I was told that I was to learn about the study of life. We were given a frog and scissors so as to cut off its head. You pity the frog. And this, in my naïve way, I sort of wondered about—the study of life? Now, I think that one of the consequences of this approach to the world, to truth, to reality, has been partly Aristotelian, in the sense that we think of truth as sliced, separated, one truth separated from another truth, and in this atomistic, this Aristotelian, logic, which is also in our blood, "a" and "not a" are separated from each other. A thing is a thing, and everything else is not that thing.

Well, there are many stupidities and mistakes and so on that come from this essentially false and incorrect notion of the truth, which more truly is holistic rather than atomistic. Ultimately the world is one and interconnected; everything is everything else as well in the very real empirical sense that we are part of each other, we're involved, and so on. And to say that I am totally separate from you is a falsehood; we're not. But that's what we've been taught since Aristotle, and that's a long time—a couple of millennia.

On Pornography

I've been involved recently with the question of the defining of pornography and of our law—that is, the business of trying to rule by law. Now, our conception of law is also Newtonian, atomistic, adversary, instead of brotherly. We need a new philosophy of law to conform with this new *weltanschauung* which is coming along. The law has the Aristotelian notion that you must define pornography in such a way that you are either on one side of the line or on the other—sharply, you know, like the national lines that are on maps. This is impossible for many things; they shade into each other. What happens is that we forget that clear pornography is very, very easily distinguishable from clear non-pornography. The difficulty lies at that point where we're trying to draw a Chinese Wall, which is exact and which is impossible to do, so that

Photo courtesy of Marcia Roltner

nobody has ever come up with a good definition of pornography. So we've given it up. And what some people then say is that there is no such thing as pornography, when what they should say is you cannot draw an Aristotelian line between pornography and non-pornography.

Now, with reference to truth, at the extremes it's very easy to tell the difference between the truth and a lie. If we focus our attention on the border areas, on the difficult cases, then we can forget that this was so and fall, for instance, into the Marxian "there is no truth." It's whatever is to the class interest and to the revolution or whatever that is useful. And then they find themselves in the situation of not being able to distinguish between the clear truth and the clear lie. If I were a newspaper reporter, I would share the conflict and the trouble they have about what exactly is the truth about something. Well, we must give up hope for what exactly is the truth, because we could be exact only about trivia.

Pornography is—I would define it for myself as—not anything that can hurt me. Some of it I am very much interested in, and some of it I like. But for the inexperienced, pornography is a fan-

48

tasy, an untruth, false expectations. These are fantasies of the kind that boys have. I can tell you one of mine. I don't mind now. I'm old enough. But here is a standard fantasy that most young boys have: they are cast away on a desert island with a whole harem of girls. Well, that's unreal in the sense that what could I have done with them? Or the fantasy that all women are nymphomaniacs. This is untrue; only two percent are. For me, this doesn't hurt, this playing with sexual thoughts, because I know the difference between reality and not-reality; but for a twelve-year-old boy it would be like telling him lies. And this is why I think that lies are something you dish out very carefully. There is a strategy of passing them along. For my daughters, now grown-up women, I would not protect them from pornography. They don't need protection. When they were ten and twelve years old and fourteen years old, they did.

Well, of course, I would love to propound only truth if that were possible—about anything and everything. Here I think it's just too personally important for the pubescent youngster. This liquid fire starts running through his veins, and this is an immediate problem. There isn't one good book on sex that I know about that has ever been written—not a true book. It's mostly crap. It's mostly messed up one way or another. The truths are mores rather than truths. We can do a hell of a lot better than has been done, and I think myself that we're moving in that direction. I think that the sexual lives of our youngsters will come closer and closer to beginning at puberty and with premarital experimentation—what they used to call companionate marriages, and so on. And I think we ought to teach them the truth, whatever we know of the truth. The total sum of sexological knowledge, by the way, is primitive. We just don't know enough. People have been too afraid to deal with the subject. So the science, in the sense of the factual knowledge about sexuality, is very sparse. But at least that ought to be passed out to the kids. I would have that kind of training and education. But that's very different from pornography. Now I might use pornography if I were teaching, let's say, a class on sex to thirteen-year-old kids. I might use it in order to teach them the difference between truth and falsehood, between what may reasonably be expected and what may not—that the male sexual fantasies are far more ambitious than his biology permits.

Photo courtesy of Marcia Roltner

Peak Experiences

I thought it was a very amusing kind of thing to extend MacGregor's Theory X and Theory Y to a Theory Z, but it turns out to be very useful, and finally I published it in *The Journal of Transpersonal Psychology* (Vol. 1, No. 2, 1969). What I have here are the generalizations from several kinds of experiences. One is from continuing work with self-actualizing people in which I discovered from one of my subjects, Eleanor Roosevelt, that she did

50

not have peak experiences. Well, when I published that stuff first, this was one exception. Everybody else reported peak experiences, so I said self-actualizing people have peak experiences. It turns out that there are more people who do not have peak experiences; and again, in a moment of being cute, I called them "peakers" and "non-peakers." And we're stuck with that vocabulary now.

The peakers are the ones who have—this is again not to make a Chinese Wall or a definite line—peak experiences sort of easily, naturally, a lot of them. And at the other end are non-peakers. I'm not sure whether they are ones who are incapable of having them or who just don't have many. So this may not be a difference in kind but rather in degree. There are many people who have peak experiences only rarely or who don't know what I mean when I'm trying to communicate with them. There is a difference between these people, if I can take them now at extremes. Aldous Huxley is a very good peaker. There are others that I could use, like Martin Buber, for instance. He is obviously a peak experiencer. All mystics in the mystical line could be called peakers. At the other extreme, non-peakers tend to be more obsessional people who are afraid of emotion anyhow and who are walling themselves off. Then, certain kinds of ideologies tend to abort peak experiences. For instance, Marxianism does. A good Marxian must not have a peak experience, because that's idealistic and counterrevolutionary. Anyway, my finding is that people who will call themselves Marxian tend not to have peak experiences. This is true also for scientists or—if I can use my nontechnical vocabulary—for tight-ass scientists. Very descriptive. Then there are others who are afraid. This I don't know enough about, but I think the schizie people or people who are afraid of being overwhelmed by emotions tend to flee from peak experiences and to interpret them in some other way. So here we have the extremes, then.

I would call peakers transcenders, because they have transcendent experiences. They are transcendent in the sense of transcending the ego, the selfish, or the skin-enclosed person. In peak experiences, when they're strong, one fuses with the world. One forgets oneself. Self-consciousness is lost. And this is a nice feeling, as you know—to be really absorbed in something, zestful about something, fascinated with something, intoxicated with something. You forget yourself, and in this sense—in this sense of the dirty ego,

51

the sense in which the Easterners call the ego a handicap on us—in peak experiences you transcend. And the most common forms—the most common triggers—come from music and from sex. These are the easiest to experience. And as you know (I don't think anybody is going to argue with me about this), that feels good. It's subjectively desirable. It's a happy state. It's a good, desirable, or positively reinforcing state.

Well, if we can take these as the pure types, then there are many things that we can learn about the future of mankind, if you'll permit me to make such a big jump all of a sudden. That is about our potentials, our possible ceilings. This can tell us something about what man may be—what is possible for him to be. These are possibilities for mankind, and any baby that is born into the world has all these as human possibilities. So this gives us, then, something about what mankind realistically and empirically may become.

The unitive consciousness, which I think we ought to know about, is very easily perceived in easy peakers: good transcenders, especially transcending self-actualizers—that is to say, psychologically healthy, fully human, highly evolved, fully matured persons. The unitive perception is one in which—as I think the Zen people may have described it best—you sacralize the ordinary. I don't know if that carries meaningfulness with it. In the person, preferably, but in a flower and tree—in anything—you can see its platonic essence at the same time that you see it as itself, in the concrete sense. It's like being reduced to the concrete, and we know the pleasures of that also. You know, the here-and-now, the Esalen or T-group kind of experiencing, of being concrete, involved in the here-and-now, of knowing what's going on at this second. But it's also being able to sacralize that concrete experience or that concrete person or that concrete thing (flower, tree, and so on).

Now, my people do that easily. It's an easy thing to do, and you can learn it. I mean this has rubbed off on me; I can do it easily. I think we can teach it, simply by force of example or by having people tell about it. And I think we can sharpen our eyes to this unitive consciousness, this unitive perception of being able to see both the secular and the sacred in every person: the here-and-now and the eternal, the archetypal, the symbolic, the mythic, the poetic, the sense in which a story is a parable also (which has far

52

greater meaning than in itself). This unitive consciousness and unitive perception are so terribly important.

Well, just to jump to the most extreme thing, this unitive perception in itself makes suicide impossible. This in itself makes life so precious. If I may say it the way I would like to say it, it makes you see the preciousness of life and the essential beauty of the trees and so on. It has very profound effects on a person because he is then living, in a certain sense, in a good world. And this can be so even in the sense of the person in physical pain or, like Aldous Huxley, dying a dignified death. This makes possible a good death, which all the religions have hoped for and tried to achieve and which is a very nice thing to have—as the existentialists have taught us—because it's quite clear that we are always suffering from this cloud that hangs over us, the fear of death. If you can transcend the fear of death, which is possible—if I could now assure you of the dignified death instead of an undignified one, of a gracious, reconciled, philosophical death (what the Catholic priest would call the good death)—your life today, at this moment, would change. And the rest of your life would change. Every moment would change. Therefore, I think we can teach this transcending of the ego, this unitive experience. As a matter of fact, I think the very fact of my few minutes of talking about it will help to bring this into consciousness for many of you so that you can keep it. It will be yours. And that's education. Therefore, since it has so many good effects, this is in a certain sense a religion-surrogate. This is one of the things that the religions have been trying to do, and, when they were successful, that's what they achieved: this unitive perception. The monks could do it. In the Christian tradition—in the Middle Ages, especially—this was taken for granted. It was possible for a monk in a monastery to say "Yes, I'm digging potatoes for the greater glory of God." And this is a meaningful thing. This means you can be whatever you are. You can be a carpenter for the greater glory of God, too. And this opens up a whole world of the sacralizing of our activities, of doing our jobs and not feeling that we're in a rat race. The kids frequently misunderstand us, you know. They think that we're caught in something when we're really caught in a love affair. They're apt not to see that we love our work. Well, this is a technique that makes possible love of your work, sacralizing your work. And that goes even for digging potatoes and for anything else.

The fact that there is a diminution in peak experiences is relevant. It's personal, but I've gotten over being shy about it, of course. I've worked it out. As you get older, peak experiences diminish. This seems to be not only my experience—which was a saddening experience—but other people's experience too. I think partly this is a self-protective device; I think that if I had the peak experiences that I had at the age of twenty or thirty or so, they would kill me. I think we're simply less strong than we were. There is a payoff, however, in that the peak experiences of the young are not always noetic—that is, they are not always cognitive; they are not always illuminative. This is very clear from the whole story of sex. Sex can be and often is peak-experiencing or "peaky." Having that quality obviously does not always mean an illumination about the world. Sometimes it does, and people can learn from sex not only that sex is beautiful but that the whole darn world is beautiful and life is beautiful and so on. One of the things that comes with age is that the cognitive elements become greater and greater as the emotional poignancy sort of slackens off and dies out. So I think— well, just simply as a personal thing—I think my subjective life is happier now than it was at the age of twenty or thirty, although I may not get all the shivers and thrills that life was full of—the first reading of a great book, or music, or girls, or babies, or flowers, or whatever—that could tear me apart in this beautiful way. What happens, then, as you grow older is (I have a name for everything) called the "plateau experience." At the age of twenty or thirty, I can remember hearing Stravinsky's *Firebird Suite* for the first time, and it half killed me. Now it doesn't half kill me; I can sit calmly and listen to it. Yet the illuminative aspects—the knowledge aspects, the sacralizing of the world—now become very easy and can be turned on and turned off just as I please. And this is a payoff of a kind. I think the good side of this whole story is that, if life goes well for you and if you use yourself well, you may confidently expect to have a better and better subjective life the older you get. I report that. The only trouble is that your goddamn body can't keep up with you. I had a German professor in college who didn't speak English very well, and he said it beautifully: the spirit is willing but the meat is feeble.

54

Leaders and Revolutionaries

The great leaders have generally been good sleepers before
the battle. It's best also to love yourself and take care of yourself
and take care of your body and, as I pointed out, to make yourself
into a better and better helper. And, if I may say it this way—if I
may think of myself as a revolutionary, as I do—I think I can be
more effective and more capable if I do not get insomnia during the
night over something that I can then do nothing about. I think that
this is wasted, foolish, self-defeating. If you have a battle, you fight
the battle. The night before the battle, the best thing to do is get a

good night's sleep and a good meal and so on—to take care of yourself.

Another free association that I get here is that I'm very much impressed with pregnant women who accept their pregnancy nicely—who like it and who develop a beautiful kind of healthy selfishness, if you know what I mean. They take care of themselves because they are the carriers of something precious.

This is one of my sadnesses about the revolutionary kids. In the first place, I think that half of them are crapping up the revolution, making it less likely and pushing it off and making it self-defeating for all the purposes that I have for and which they say that they have for peace and brotherhood and universal love. They try to achieve this by hatred and cracking your skull in and divisiveness. If you don't mind, when I feel good, I snicker at it, and when I feel bad, I get very depressed. I think that there are lessons for the one who wants to change the world, to improve the world.

I don't want to use the word *revolutionary* because we'll fight over meanings of it. I consider myself a revolutionary, and I consider most of the kids who talk with me as making the true revolution far less likely. You know, "Protect me from my friends, please."

If you're a general, so to speak, that's one thing; if you're a corporal, that's another thing. For the general—for the one in charge—it is very, very desirable not to be overwhelmed by his emotions. It's best to be cool and calm instead of feeling embittered or angry or guilty. Corporals and sergeants can permit themselves to be terribly impassioned. A good general—five-star-general revolutionary—had better be cool. He'll simply come out with better decisions and be less likely to lead his troops over the edge of a cliff.

Part Three

John Donne from Devotions

. . .

No man is an Island, entire of it selfe;
Every man is a piece of the Continent, a part of the maine;
If a Clod bee washed away by the Sea, Europe is the lesse,
As well as if a Promontory were,
As well as if a Manor of thy friends or of thine own were.
Any man's death diminishes me, because I am involved in
  Mankinde,
And therefore never send to know for whom the bell tolls,
It tolls for thee.

. . .

This can be used nicely as is to apply to the B-realm.* If it is diminished, I am diminished, and so is everyone else—whether or not he is aware of it.

* Being-realm

59

Maslow's Contract with the W. P. Laughlin
Charitable Foundation, March 1969*

My plans and hopes for my work under the grant from the Laughlin Foundation had better be separately specified under "immediate" and "long-term." My grand life-long plan is to construct and write the comprehensive and systematic psychology and philosophy of human nature and society, which is now already in the process of formation. This humanistic psychology is in the truest sense a *general* and comprehensive outlook on life, a world view or life philosophy that is not merely intellectual but is also a way of living; a system of ethics and values, of politics and economics, of education and religion; a philosophy of science, and so on. A new image of man and a new image of society generate changes in all aspects of human life and in all the social institutions that are, after all, products of human nature. These new possibilities (or probabilities) are revolutionary in almost the same sense that the Darwinian revolution was—or the Freudian, Newtonian, and Einsteinian revolutions were.

This is the general structure at which I've been working for twenty-five years or so and within which I've been constructing one piece after another, each of which fitted into the general plan at one place or another. And this is my plan for the rest of my life also. That is, while keeping the overall structure in mind always, I shall work from day to day at the separate building blocks that are needed to complete the general psychology.

For the immediate future—that is to say, during the next few years—I intend to work up the philosophy of democratic politics, economics, and ethics that is generated by the humanistic psychology and that is exemplified—but not yet explicitly—in the so-called Eupsychian Network—such organizations as NTL (National Training Laboratories), Esalen, Synanon. I have pushed this forward in priority because of the current assault on American values and loss of faith in them. I believe it can be demonstrated

* Now the International Study Project, Inc.

60

that the most basic of these democratic values are inherent in the structure of human nature itself (as seen by the humanistic psychologies) and need not rest solely on blind faith or tradition or habit. From my point of view as a psychologist, I interpret much of the current turmoil, especially among the young, as an anguished cry for just such values—something to believe in that is also intellectually and scientifically respectable.

Some necessary subaspects of this job, all of which I am working at right now (in some cases with collaborators), are (1) a demonstration of the biological roots and nature of these values, which I shall publish as my presidential paper for the American Psychological Association; (2) a brief and informal book on Humanistic education; (3) a compilation of my recent writings into a book to be called *The Farther Reaches of Human Nature*, the most important of which is an investigation that finds the higher motivations of the healthiest individuals to be what have been called the eternal verities, the spiritual values, and so on; (4) a psychological and scientific examination of the "problem of evil" and its necessary place in the humanistic ethic; (5) a study of the effects of humanistic psychology on the black-white situation and on intergroup relations in general; (6) an investigation of the various ways in which the active agent differs from the passive pawn, which involves reevaluating our notions of will, responsibility, determinism, and the like; (7) a study of some of the implications for social, institutional, and organizational change of this enlarged conception of human nature. There are others I hope to get to sooner or later which I shall not detail.

I have already spelled out the values for science of this new psychology in a book called *The Psychology of Science*. I am now working away at a similar book on education in which I hope to help supply a more adequate philosophy and practice of education than are now available—one that is easily deducible from the new psychologies.

This whole enterprise started around 1940 as "a psychology for the peace table." I still feel that world peace is not possible until we all know about the higher potentials of man, as well as his lowest. But today I feel, even more ambitiously, that we begin to know enough, not only about achieving peace, but also about how to live after it is achieved.

61

1922

1929

1929

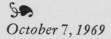
October 7, 1969

Humanistic psychology is essentially empirical and scientific in the sense of (a) the humble recognition of not knowing enough; (b) the expectation or faith that in part the salvation of mankind lies in the advancement of knowledge; (c) the Socratic notion that the advancement of knowledge—especially of persons—automatically improves human and social values; (d) the idea that knowledge can improve in reliability, validity, pertinence, exactness, and in holistic interconnection and relevance.

1964

I am a new breed—a theoretical psychologist parallel to theoretical physicists or, even better, to theoretical biologists (because the latter actually *do* lab work, or *did*). In one way this is different from the example of William James and John Dewey, who turned to philosophy from psychology, because they were never researchers and I was (I am). I think of myself as a scientist rather than an essayist or philosopher. I feel myself very bound to and by the facts that I am trying to *perceive*, not to create. My creations are structures or organizations of facts. I neither feel free, nor ever *want* in any way, to leave them. I want to describe them and organize and communicate what I see.

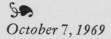
November 4, 1969

I can tell you it's a tough life, all full of anxiety attacks, nightmares, depressions, conflicts, and uncertainties. There is a huge abyss between feeling intuitively, subjectively certain or convinced *and* having the courage to say it, without any real evidence, to a cold-eyed nonbeliever, a skeptical scientist who asks for proof, or at least for data, or at *least* for logic.

63

The essential word is *courage*—nerve, brass, chutzpah—at least for opening one's mouth and even more for committing yourself to print. Of course *everybody* functions by intuition in part, or at least everybody has this possibility. Many don't dare to express it (even though they act on it), but I suppose there are many who don't even let it become conscious and who think of the "wild surmise" as a trap, a danger, an inner whisper from the devil.

And then the yearning is great to get back to safe ground, to solid data, to variables that you can define nicely, to behavior that you can see with your own eyes, to a delimited problem with boundary conditions within which you can work away happily in an untroubled way, forging ahead steadily and surely. I could have stayed with my monkeys. Indeed, I *would* have, only I had no monkeys and no lab when I left Wisconsin. Or I could even have stayed with the sexological researches, which fascinated me, which were obviously important, and which were like untouched gold mines for the researcher, as Kinsey later found out. I was starting on extensive studies of prostitutes and of male and female homosexuals about the time the war started.

But I gave it all up in favor of historical urgency, or constructing a psychology "for the peace table," which then looked to be 30–40 years away. (My *Abnormal Psychology* started out to be a chapter in this big, general philosophy of human nature, which I've been writing all my life.) I felt more or less consciously discontented with academic psychology (although I also loved it and was fascinated by it). Behavioristic, laboratory, conventional, *Psychological-Abstracts* stuff would clearly be too slow to help make a new and better world and to teach people to love each other, or at least to be kind rather than hostile or cruel.

I got all involved in SPSSI (Society for the Psychological Study of Social Issues) and helped to get it organized. This was certainly one obvious path. I was convinced that what we needed against the depression, prejudice, and war were *facts*—truth, data, science. But clearly not science as it was then. It had to change its direction, its problems, its attitudes, its philosophy. We could study "learning," as it was laughingly called (rats in mazes, nonsense syllables, conditioning—while Katona's revolutionary book was neglected and went out of print), for a thousand years and it would do us no good ethically, socially, philosophically. It seemed to me

64

akin to picking at one's old scabs or the like, a kind of group auto-eroticism (to which I likened it—masturbation in the laboratory).

I spent a whole summer (the one before the atom bomb) at Sabbathday Lake in Maine, writing up—or, rather, condensing—huge piles of notes on the shortcomings of conventional science and scientists (paper published in 1946). My conclusion was, in effect, that it was the timid scientists who fell short rather than science itself, which had greater possibilities for human and social emancipation than had been used.

I learned later in psychoanalysis that much of my push and my change in direction came out of being the object of anti-Semitism (and also, therefore, of being especially horrified by anti-Negroism).

I can now say it (and I see it) much more clearly than I did then. I simply didn't *understand* anti-Semitism. It seemed to me like a totally mysterious, unexplainable, unpredictable, whimsical kind of ailment that seized on people in a mysterious way. I simply couldn't understand it, let alone predict it or control it.

I am sure that my preoccupation with the inner intricacies of human nature, and especially of mental health and illness and of social health and illness, led me to the search for values and ethics and to an interest in psychotherapy and social therapy (Utopianism). Furthermore, I think this is peculiarly Jewish, and it may yet become peculiarly Negro. The whole enterprise is a kind of huge coping mechanism (rather than defense), a way of fighting depression, inferiority feelings, self-hatred, lowering of self-esteem, feelings of lovelessness and of being unloveworthy.

&❧

The One-Way Membrane

One great advantage of being a Jew—an advantage that many do not appreciate or are not even aware of—is that you are automatically exempted from contact with anti-Semites.

Because I am a Jew, I carry with me always a semipermeable membrane that has the miraculous property of excluding from contact with me bores, dolts, mean people, sadists, stuffed shirts, the overconventionalized anti-Semites, Fascists, and other such undesirable people. But this does not exclude *all* non-Jews. The only Christians I ever get to know well are the decent, honorable, brotherly, and friendly people.

Coming into a new community, especially in a small town [1947], this has been of incalculable importance to me. I have been almost completely spared the whole dreary round of ceremonial visits from preachers, American Legionnaires, sewing circles, benevolent orders, fraternal orders, various dull neighbors, etc. I have not been invited to the usual tea parties, ceremonial calls, or afternoons of chit-chat that take so much of the time of the ordinary person. I have not been summoned to those formal dinners at which hours are spent making superficial comments on this and that with various strangers one will never see again.

In a word, I have been spared the worst half of the culture—the stereotyped, the dull, the boring, the ceremonial. I am exempted from routine waste of time with the worst half of the American population, the sick minds, the overtimid, the profoundly hostile, with whom, if I were not a Jew, I should have to fritter away so large a proportion of my precious hours. I have never known well a Fascist or a Nazi or even a native reactionary.

Thus it comes about that the only unpleasant or nasty or boring people I know well are Jews. My membrane doesn't work for them. This is also true for Communists. Here, too, my membrane loves its selective ability.

Although I do not know directly of my own knowledge, my strong guess is that something of the sort must also be true for blacks. Perhaps it is even *more* true for them than for Jews. And it would be interesting to find out how it is for Orientals, Latin Americans, Indians, etc.

§◗

1965

It's just that I haven't got the time to do careful experiments myself. They take too long, in view of the years that I have left and the extent of what I want to do.

So I myself do only "quick-and-dirty" little pilot explorations, mostly with a few subjects only, inadequate to publish but

66

enough to convince myself that they are probably true and will be confirmed one day. Quick little commando raids, guerrilla attacks.

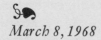

March 8, 1968

Well, if I can transcend the jungle by getting up above it and looking down calmly, then in principle I can climb up above the human species itself as if I were nonhuman, a God, a Martian, or, better, a human being in his divine moments, in B-cognition, looking from above at himself below, as one does on the psychoanalytic couch. I can then look at human beings, pushing aside my identification, my interests, my stake in them. I can be the Kibitzer and not be involved in losing or winning money in the poker game. (It's harder to be *in* the poker game and be emotionless, fearless, about losing or winning money.) And if I can't actually *do* it, then at least I can conceive it—that I should perceive for the moment nonhumanly, superhumanly, the whole human species. I can certainly imagine that the species would kill itself. Then nature would remain. That's easy enough to do. In the same way I can imagine this "nature remaining with the human species left in."

Then I also thought of using this in my president's address [to APA] to say "we are all Messiahs, we psychologists." There aren't any others. Use Pope John story: "Sometimes half-asleep I think of some reform or improvement and say to myself 'I must tell the Pope about that.' And then I start up suddenly as I realize 'But *I* am the Pope.' " *We* have the responsibility for understanding all these things, proving them, studying them, researching them, and getting firmer and firmer knowledge about them.

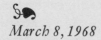

Undated Note

Many of the greatest discoveries in psychology have come from outside academic psychology, from psychiatrists and physiologists mostly, but also from philosophers and educators. The history of academic, "scientific" psychology is largely a saddening story of futility and of very careful and painstaking exploration of one blind alley after another.

This is not due to the fact that academic psychologists are an inferior species. I am quite sure they are as intelligent and capable a group as any other. Their disease is their immature conception of science. I sometimes think they would be far better off if the word *science* had never been invented. It is an amazing thing to see what happens to an ordinary, well-intentioned human being when he enlists in the APA (for example, "the self-castration, the narrowing down of the world"). "Science" for such a man seems to be regarded largely as an excluding and denying function (for example, "That is an unscientific problem." "That is mystical, mentalistic." "That is religion." "Give up philosophy, art, poetry.") It seems sometimes to be like a permanent Lent, defined largely in terms of giving up, renouncing, sacrificing, narrowing down.

Undated Note

In a very general way, we are justified in making a crude differentiation between using science for safety purposes and using it for growth purposes. Or, to say it in another way, also oversimple but also useful, the search for knowledge can be instigated by the desire to allay fear *or* it can be an expression of courage. Since the two kinds of science that are generated by these two psychological origins are extremely different, and since it is my thesis that we need more of growth-science and less of safety-science, it will help to turn to an exposition of the psychodynamics of safety and of growth in the individual.

Undated Note

Then I tried to tell W. that, whenever I started something, I gave up the inhibiting effects of logic, proof, reliability, and so on, and all the cautions and criticisms of my careful and critical friends

68

University of Wisconsin, 1934

Rocky Mountain Park, Colorado, August 1933

University of Wisconsin, 1934

University of Wisconsin, 1933

and dashed on ahead into the wilderness, trusting myself and my intuitions. Otherwise I'd never do anything (except criticize the doers, just as G. has done. He's so aware of the possible mistakes that he's paralyzed and has never fulfilled his capacities and been fruitful—like others who are more dashing and daring and no more intelligent). I remember the letter I wrote once to Eliseo Vivas, replying in the only way possible to his very just and sound criticisms and cautions about tangling experimentally with the philosophical questions and difficulties (it would take two lifetimes to study everything and be perfectly scholarly before beginning the research). I told him I understood what he was saying, but "I would be determinedly naïve" (that is, not just go ahead and get wet, by plunging into the water, even if it wasn't lighted and I might crack my skull). Can a cautious man attack an unexplored wilderness or swamp? In research training, I told G., we all act on this by urging our students to plunge *in* and get wet with actual research. The criticism from within the circle of researchers who have gotten wet is so different from the criticisms of the spectators in the stands.

What I kept trying to tell W. was that he was too vulnerable and too responsive to applause and criticism from below his level. To be on top of Mount Olympus *means* loneliness—very few people to talk with. But one has to be lofty and compassionate and also be affectionate and friendly.

§

Undated Note

Primary processes: how best to release them? Don't try, strain. Don't be eager. Be interested to see what idea develops. Not too goal-oriented (then your eye is on the goal, not on the matter in hand). Become unmotivated. Not too reality-oriented. Close out the world. Loaf, laze, enjoy.

The best way to catch a dog is not to go running after him. Don't anticipate the future (avoid future mistakes, foreboding, apprehension, worry).

Don't turn back to the past. Don't go into your memory. If anything in the past is relevant, it will be part of your present self (integrated with it rather than discrete, undigested, unintegrated, separate, isolated piece).

Give up logic, rationality, order, linearity, secondary elaboration, time schedules.

Give up criticism, editing.

Permit anything to come into consciousness. Acceptance (no irrelevance, obscenity, craziness, irrationality, impossibility, and so on).

Watch the movie (receptive, passive, let-be, trust). Give up control. Let happen whatever will happen.

§•

August 17, 1955

I think I can sum up my feelings about psychoanalysis, pro and con, in the following statements.

1. Freud has supplied us with the best psychotherapy we have. Including its improvements in recent years, along with its revisions and variants, there is not even a near second available.

2. It is so far also our best system of psychopathology. This is true for pathogeneses and for classification as well as for dynamics. Even its characterology, though primitive and undeveloped, is useful for the therapist trying to cure psychological illness.

3. However, it is quite unsatisfactory as a general psychology of the whole human being, especially in his healthier and more admirable aspects. The picture of man it presents is a lopsided, distorted puffing up of his weaknesses and shortcomings that purports then to describe him fully. This it clearly fails to do. Practically all the activities that man prides himself on, and that give meaning, richness, and value to his life, are either omitted or pathologized by Freud. Work, play, love, art, creativeness, religion in the good sense, ethics, philosophy, science, learning, parenthood, self-sacrifice, heroism, saintliness, goodness—these are all weakly handled, if at all.

71

1964

I've gotten into so many discussions of this for myself and my relations to Freud. Then I explain that *I* am carrying on in the spirit of Freud—*not* the psychoanalysts, who are merely pious and loyal. I try to tell them that I can take it all for granted. I have eaten it all and digested it and have made it into my flesh, which it now is. But I am eager for the next meal. I am not content to regurgitate and chew and rechew on the same cud. I've already gotten the nourishment out of it, discarded the nonnutritious parts, and then gone on to building something myself.

1964

Stimulated by a question from Frederich Weiss in New York City about relations between Freudian psychodynamics and existentialism, I reacted, in a very strong and decided way, that I thought the latter without the former could be a real danger, a superstructure without a foundation, a Pollyanna theology without end, a loss of depth and roots. I feel the same about Tao, Zen, and other "merely hopeful" psychologies. They are "high ψ" without the "lower ψ." When hierarchically integrated with their lower foundations, which make them possible, they are the highest ceiling; without the foundations, they are illusions and fantasies.

November 23, 1960

Dear Dr. _____:

I am very disappointed with your paper on early memory, just as I was somewhat disappointed with your previous mimeographed work on psychological health. What I am afraid of for you is the complete parochialism that is so common in medically trained psychoanalysts and that I had hoped the academically trained psy-

72

chologists could avoid. You have completely overlooked the rich Adlerian literature on early memory. For instance, I remember one excellent paper by Heinz Ansbacher. Your footnote on page 508 is not only inadequate but also snotty and shows the usual contempt with which an orthodox analytic group treats all outsiders and strangers. I may agree with you that Adler's explanatory concepts were limited, and I may agree with you that Freud was easily the greatest psychologist who ever lived; yet a science is not made up of one leader and a lot of stooges or loyal devotees.

I urge you to think of the young psychoanalysts as your colleagues, collaborators, and partners and not as spies, traitors, and wayward children. You can never develop a science that way—only an orthodox church.

Your colleague,
A. H. Maslow, Chairman
Department of Psychology

P.S. It occurs to me that a good way of saying what I want to say is that I consider myself as Freudian as you but not as *exclusively* Freudian.

§๏

July 16, 1968

    An article by Henry Winthrop in the *Journal of Existentialism* reminds me that I must get to work sooner or later on making explicit the underlying philosophy that is implicit to the Eupsychian Network. I think Winthrop makes a mistake when he speaks about high culture and middle-brow culture, because this ties the whole business to a completely outworn class structure. It's one characteristic of the new Eupsychian Ethic that it is class-free and has no class lines. Also defense-free. An important point in this ethic is to have transcended the fear of unpopularity, ostracism, of being cast out of the group. This is a transcendence of belongingness in favor of truth, honesty, authenticity. Some distinction will eventually have to be made between the third level and the fourth level—that is, between humanistic and transpersonal.

So far as validation and science and proof are concerned, I would have to add that the whole philosophy rests on love of life or a valuing of life. If anybody says "Why should I not commit suicide? Life has no value for me," then there is no real answer to be made to him; the whole humanistic and transpersonal and Eupsychian philosophies and psychologies are worthless for him. That is, stress that the whole structure of thinking rests upon being life-positive. It is actually from the descriptive point of view, what a Martian would observe of self-actualizing people and peakers. This is not an "ought" philosophy, and it should not be sold as such.

Add also the important point that I've already made in my Existentialism paper, of the tragic sense of life, of seriousness, of depth in contrast to the shallowness, the living on the surface, the confinement to the momentary and the concrete, and to the here-now in the bad sense. Look up the other stuff in my Existentialism paper and also in the Existential sections in my *Eupsychian Management*. There are other distinctions to be added.

Consider Sinnott's sense of the necessity for a universalistic philosophy that all human beings could adhere to and that then, of course, would bind them together into one species, which would then make more possible One World and a One-World Government. This means, of course, paying no serious attention to differences of religion or race or nationality or anything else that is peripheral and superficial. The only thing that is basic and central is human specieshood. Once this is accepted, then all the other differences can be accepted in a cultural pluralism or a racial pluralism or a religious pluralism without doing any harm and actually enriching life. But when they serve as walls to cut human beings off from each other, or to cut the human species into walled-off subspecies, then of course they are very dangerous and frightening and have to be destroyed.

§❧

January 9, 1968

I have a good way of integrating my critique of the culture with my admiration for it and for identification and patriotism. I

74

think I'll call it the American Dream and the American Nightmare and then list them side by side. Then it won't *sound* Pollyanna *or* nihilistic, optimistic *or* pessimistic, but will get the whole picture.

Undated Note

The concept of SA (self-actualization) has been consistently misunderstood and misread and misused both by scholars and by laymen, especially young ones. By the scholar it has often been dismissed as "optimistic" wish-fulfillment or as strictly unworthy of a scientist. Granted that this was a "first-stage" investigation, having all the faults of any beginning. Yet I have been able to wonder at the "scientists" who demand that truths be born equipped with a full set of teeth. To demand rigor, exactness, detail from a first exploration of a wilderness is just plain silly, and I've refused to be apologetic about discovering a gold mine.

April 1, 1963

3:15 A.M. Can't sleep. Will try catching fleeting thoughts and writing them down instead of waiting for them to grow into something. One good way of using insomnia time.

Epi-Freudian means, or will mean from now on, building upon Freud. Not repudiating, not fighting, not either-or, not loyalties or counter-loyalties. Just taking for granted his clinical discoveries, psychodynamics, etc., insofar as true. Using them, building upon them the superstructure which they lack. This does not involve swallowing any of his mistakes.

Perhaps same for behaviorism and positivism and simple-minded scientism. Maybe epi-positivism because I want to save this empirical, testing, checking, conservative emphasis. But also I want to build upon it because a negative checking and continuousness amount to nothing in themselves—worse than nothing. Actually a real superstructure, higher ceilings, Third Force can give behaviorism some worth and some usefulness—that is, can "use" it.

February 1940

Spring 1943

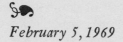

February 5, 1969

These are notes that I have thought of as a possibility for a paper for a mass-circulation magazine. I have thought about it for some years now, but I just have no taste for popular writing and I always avoid the job. But now it occurs to me again that first of all I must, I should, do it. Nobody else is doing it. That's what started me off this morning—finishing Manuel's book on Newton, where he leaves off as if the humanistic science didn't exist. Then in the conversation here, the good thought occurred to me to make a lecture out of it or a chapter in the Propositions book. That's what I think I'll do. I think I'll begin the next semester, the first lecture, on the revolution. And what was running through my mind was that these disgusting magazines all indicate the alienation of the whole intellectual establishment and their lack of knowledge of the new beginnings of intellectual synthesis which they don't even know about. And then I was thinking this morning: where are the great names from among the humanists? These magazines never mention them. Where are Carl Rogers and Gordon Allport and Harry Murray and Gardner Murphy, let alone the younger ones like Mike Murphy, for instance? Why did not Manuel include or go on to the post-Newtonian synthesis in science with Polanyi and my book and stuff like that? Why aren't the books that the humanistic psychologists write ever mentioned, let alone the writings of the relatively few humanistic sociologists, economists, politics people, philosophers? Their books aren't noticed. For instance, none of my books have ever been noticed in any popular magazine.

One sad thing about the whole business is that you can interpret one aspect of the radical youth rebellion and of the Negro rebellion as reaching out for this very humanistic entranced personal ethic and philosophy. They reach out for it as if it didn't exist. And yet it does exist. They just don't know about it. You could call it in a way an answer to their prayers, to their demands. In principle it is something that should satisfy them, because it's a system of values that involves a reconstruction of science as a means of discovering and uncovering values (rather than it being value-free). Not only that, it includes the beginnings of a strategy

77

in tactics of reaching there—that is, a theory of education, including a philosophy of education including both means and ends of education. The same thing for politics and economics. That is, one can talk about moral politics or Eupsychian or humanistic politics and economics, and divide this discussion into one of ultimate goals and intrinsic values on the one hand, and then strategy and tactics and means on the other hand. If I wanted to, and had the time, I could include also the theory of B-art—that is, of art as exposing the realm of Being, of producing peak experiences and plateau experiences, of improving the human being or at least of exposing to him the ideal world that is possible for him to attain. Something of the sort could be said for music also, as in my paper on music education. There is hardly any philosopher whom I could refer to here except in bits and pieces. But then this whole thing that I'm writing itself constitutes a comprehensive philosophy of life. That philosophy or psychology of B-art should include also poetry, the novel, the drama, the verbal arts as having the same goals and the same strategy and tactics, the same intrinsic values, the same trans-personal usefulness for mankind. That is, art in general can be seen as a growth-fostering technique, a self-actualizing and humanness-fulfilling path. We raise the question here of statistics in the population—that is, of how many people are touched now by this new synthesis and how many people would be touched by it, supposing there were publicity and supposing there were statements in mass-circulation magazines and the TV and the radio. The answer from history is pretty clear: you can expect that it would be the 1 percent in this generation reaching out to the 1 percent in the next generation. That is, you would expect in advance that the whole business would be wrapped around with the normal amount of misunderstanding and misinterpretation and confusion. But this is inevitable. The growing-tip is a small proportion of mankind. They will carry on. As a matter of fact, that is what is happening with the whole humanistic synthesis now; the groundbreaking is done by a few people, and most of the stuff is just routine or mediocre or positive crap. That's all part of the game, and there is no avoiding it as long as human beings are human beings.

One big point is that whatever the statistics may turn out to be for the pace with which this point of view is supported and validated and accepted, it is still terribly important that it just exists, because this is the antidote against hopelessness and against the hopeless pessimism of the kind that exists in so very many people of the intellectual class of both the older and the younger ones. These people who just wind up in despair and just see no way out. All they can do is criticize and protest, and they see no hopefulness for positive reconstruction and transcending syntheses that go beyond what exists now. This is what I mean partly by the "growing-tip" in the next generation and in nonpsychological groups in this generation: to give them the vision of at least a possibility, if not a certainty, that there is a leap forward that is possible, that there is a theory of social improvement or revolution, that there is the possibility of envisaging a good society. It is not true that society must inevitably be bad, as the anarchists think it must be. Nor is it inevitable, as so many theologians and "theologians of left radicals and right radicals" say, that human nature must be evil and can never be good, can never grow into anything better. The humanistic and transpersonal synthesis knocks these ideas on the head, or at least contradicts them. I would guess that the more jestful and cheerful and life-positive and hopeful and optimistic people now existing and to exist in the next generation would seize upon this new revolution, even though it is not yet verified sufficiently. And then they would act on it, they would live by it, they would work at it. And of course that's what it needs —workers, in all the fields, both scientific and professional and applied. And of course something like this is needed in the recesses of one's open private subjective mind in order to give one the courage and hope to go on and to work toward something better.

It can be stressed that this whole humanistic synthesis is like a smorgasboard, a big table containing all sorts of ways of life and paths of life and interests. Then each individual would choose that particular path of life which struck him and which accorded with his interests and his perceptions and his tastes. Thus art would certainly not work for everybody. It would leave blind people cold, but it would work for some people who were especially sensitive. The same thing would be true for the mesomorphic way of athletics of the body—of dancing, for instance—rather than visual art. There are after all many B-values, and anyone can enter into the B-realm via any single one of the B-values—via the search for beauty or for truth or for virtue, perfection, law, order, or whatever it might be.

§•

1970

The affirmation of the rooting of the psyche in the body in biology is a repudiation of the strictly cultural or historical or existential explanation of psychology. From the existential point of view, this is an affirmation of biological essentialism. The human psyche is *not* solely a product of our immersion in existential situations ("rooted in the conditions of existence"). Man has great freedom, certainly, but not total freedom. He must pay, and pay heavily, for any repudiation of his biological nature and for any avoidance of his biological fate. He does create himself in large part, but from given possibilities (not from nothing).

It also implies a repudiation of any dichotomizing of the mind and the body or of flesh and spirit or of higher nature and lower nature.

§•

June 4, 1970

The more I think of the Eupsychian Society, the more I realize how profoundly involved I was and how much affected by the social anthropology that I discovered in Madison in about 1932 or so when I first read Malinowski, Mead, Benedict, and Linton. For me this was all a tremendous revelation, and I went around lecturing at the psychology classes of various instructors about this new dispensation for psychology. I was convinced that psychology had been ethnocentric. I decided for myself to be a part-time anthropologist because that was sine qua non for being a good psychologist. Otherwise you were simply a naïve local. And I remember lecturing everybody else about it too.

80

It was during this time that I prepared and wrote what was probably the first essay on personality and culture by any psychologist. This was a chapter for Ross Stagner's book *Psychology of Personality* (McGraw-Hill, 1937). I had written this material some years before it finally appeared and had huge quantities of it. The chapter I wrote for Stagner was very much boiled down and selected from large amounts of writing that I had done.

This revelation was successor to one that happened to me in my sophomore year, when I read William Graham Sumner's *Folkways*. I stumbled across this book by the sheerest accident. I had registered at City College for a course entitled Philosophy of Civilization, to be taught by Morris Raphael Cohen, whom I had heard much of and wanted to study with. When I showed up in class, I learned that Cohen was off on a sabbatical and that A. B. was taking his place. He assigned Sumner as *the* textbook for the course. I never did discover what the hell B. was talking about. Partly, it was too difficult for me. I just wasn't educated enough then. But partly, also, he is a chaotic thinker (I now know), and I still don't know what the hell he's talking about. In any case, at that time of course I blamed it on myself and dropped the course. But because I got fascinated with Sumner, this was probably one of the most important courses I ever took.

I nibbled away at Sumner, not quite understanding it. I kept coming back to it again and again, and one night there was a big breakthrough of awe, admiration. It was a kind of cold chill and hair-standing-on-end peak experience—not just happy but also mixed in with vows, with a certain sense of the uncanny, with a feeling of littleness and incapability and the like. The point was that the vow—that's what it would have been called 500 years ago —was also a resolution (as my ethnocentrism dropped away like old clothes, and as I became a citizen of the world in that one evening) to do like Sumner. For some reason that I can't fathom now, I swore to myself that I would try to, or that I *would*, make this kind of contribution to philosophy, to psychology, and to anthropology. Why these three I don't remember. If I had been in King Arthur's Court, I suppose I would have kept vigil beside my sword and before the altar all night long. But that was exactly the spirit of it. In any case, that's what I've done.

Philadelphia, May 1958

Brooklyn College, 1950 (photo courtesy of Arthur Schatz)

1957

First year at Brandeis, 1951

1965

I've noticed in myself a deliberate effort to husband my in-dignation—that is, *not* to shout off at every evil, or fight every battle—because I want so much time for my life work, for my per-sonal life, and for seeking whatever enjoyment I can in the last por-tion of my life. That is, I try to do a good and full job with a *few* things and try to harden myself against all the rest, trying *not* to get involved, not to get angry, etc. It's a different kind of psychic housekeeping—with limited energy, with limited years left, and with positive responsibilities of all kinds that the youngsters don't have. They can go gung-ho for anything that turns up on the hori-zon. I can't.

I guess this *also* adds up to better knowledge of the D-realm,* *not* to giving up the B-realm.

Another thought: I wonder if this youthful rebelliousness and its shortcomings can also be seen under the head of the "fruitful psychosis" or the "positive disintegration"—the breaking up of an old pattern in order to make way for a new and better one. There is a total and violent repudiation of what was totally accepted only a few years earlier. Is this like the parallel child's total love of the parents and then the later repudiation of this love?

This is still confusing.

1965

Can we improve the communication between the B- and the D-realms—between the young idealists and their more politic elders? This kind of phrasing may help the kids to respect the politicism. The man pressing toward the same B-values as fast as he can—which can't be very fast. I wonder if my theory of slow revolution will get around, and, if so, will it help? If only the kids could stick to their own guns and *yet* also respect the practical politicians. And also if the practical-politician adults could respect

*Deficiency-realm

83

and like and appreciate the impatience of the young and their perfectionism as coming partly from simple lack of knowledge and experience with the D-world. It's so hard to love an adolescent, but it has to be achieved.

I've also had the feeling that the good youngsters react very violently against all the TV crap hypocrisy and creeping evil. The same on radio, public and official speeches, etc. Maybe they react more intensely than the elders do. Partly negative adaptation, partly familiarization, partly deliberate defenses against getting involved or getting angry, partly greater knowledge of how all this TV shit is tied into so many aspects of the whole culture that it's almost an insurmountable job to defeat.

ৡ৲

November 13, 1969

It's more clear in my mind that *the* great distinction—the really important one for Social Psychology, Politics, the Evil folder, etc.—is the distinction between the Responsibles and all others. Partly this is the Agent-Pawn distinction, except that Pawn is not the only antonym to Agent or to Responsible. There are other opposites as well; clearly one such specific group is the Non-experienced. This includes young people generally, but it also includes older perfectionists and B-monsters who demand the pure, the perfect, the unflawed, and who turn against flaws as if they were totally evil.

This calls for a careful distinction among idealists; the responsible ones (practical, realistic, constructive) and the irresponsible ones (perfectionists, the sick ones in the Freudian sense, destructivists, nihilists), the ones who could never conceivably be satisfied by anything actual because it can never live up to the perfect fantasies in their heads—the perfect human, the perfect society, the perfect marriage, the perfect teacher, etc.

Include another angle on the SDS types, the New Left, etc. —namely, that their refusing to do anything until a perfect society is attained and their complaining about the overwhelming forces in the society as a justification for not getting involved, for not taking on jobs, for not helping, are themselves other forms of being a

84

Pawn. What it amounts to is saying "I am absolutely helpless because society is so overwhelmingly stronger than I am, and it's so overwhelmingly evil, that it would prevent me from being good." The upshot is: doing nothing, achieving nothing. Deep down, I think, nobody trusts this type—even the ones who follow them. Nobody would dream of marrying such a man and having children with him. I think everybody feels that he is not a responsible human being and that good interpersonal relations with him are simply impossible.

Include in the total picture the inexperience of youth. That is to say, the nonexperience of the inexperienced: they haven't married, so they've never had to learn how to get along with a woman (certainly a great education); they haven't had children to be responsible for; they haven't had to meet bills on time, to make budgets; they haven't learned what it's like to get fired or promoted. Perhaps I'll try one day, if I have the time, to work up more carefully the whole concept of immaturity to include all the ways in which there are levels of cognitive development, emotional development, development of realism and reality testing and the like. I think finally that it's a mistake to call them, as I did, stupid. This has other implications. It would be best to say immature or inexperienced, in a cool, calm way detailing just what is meant.

I used to love higher IQs and brilliance much more than I do now. As I get older, I seem to value character and responsibility more than I do IQs.

The world seemed generally to be run by an upper 5–10 percent of managerial types whom now I think I would call, rather, the Responsible Persons—the ones you can count on, the ones with a sense of duty, the ones whose word you can trust. Now of course this is a matter of degree, ranging from the fraction of 1 percent of aggridants like Bill Laughlin on down. Yet whatever the percentage, and however shadowy the line may be between Responsibles and Nonresponsibles, the gap is huge, almost as between two species. The more I think of it, the more I must make of it.

But it now looks as if I'd better add on for basic relevance that the Eupsychian Philosophy is essentially for, of, and by Responsibles.

Yesterday I stressed (at the University of Santa Clara)—more than usual, but I think in a good way—the limitations of my data, the "gold-medal wearers." I think it's best to be modest about the applicability of my data. It's clear already that they apply to more mature people and perhaps also to Responsibles. What are the limitations, then, of the data? This is an empirical question. Is my Eupsychian Philosophy not applicable to the immature, the life-negative, the Nonresponsibles? Or is it less applicable, or partially applicable? How about Dr. Charlotte Bühler's dependent types? How about the constitutionally weak, sick, passive, crippled, brain-injured, etc.? Perhaps I'd better make more explicit that I am describing an ideal type and then *assuming* that it may apply to all other human beings.

It occurs to me that many of the militants can be classified simply as projecting blame entirely outward: you are not to blame for any of your own miseries; you must lay all the blame on society. Of course, this is self-defeating or self-destructive. One can spend a lifetime assigning blame, finding the causes "out there" for all troubles that exist. Contrast this with the "responsible attitude" of confronting the situation, bad or good, and, instead of asking "What caused the trouble? Who was to blame?" asking "How can I handle this present situation best to make the most of it? What can I salvage here?"

Sა

Undated Note

"The miseries of Asia are a fearful page in history. Her people found strength to endure by denying any meaning and any importance to what they could not escape. Ages ago in India, the world of the reason and the world of the spirit were divorced and the universe handed over to the latter."

These are techniques for avoiding the harsh truth—if it is harsh enough. It *must* then be avoided. This shows that we must have a good world and good conditions for truth to be beautiful and to be attractive and for us to have faith in it.

Under these good conditions, dispassionate objectivity is itself a passion (for the *real* and for the truth). Call it conative curiosity (it is both cognitive and conative simultaneously). Add to this a preference and a taste for the real rather than for the unreal

86

and for the true rather than for the false. Plus the fact that peak experiences can come from the truth.

Intellect, reason, and curiosity equal a passion to know reality out there, partly to relieve inner anxiety but partly also for growth, for peak experiences, because reality is so beautiful.

If you love the truth, you'll trust it—that is, you will expect it to be good, beautiful, perfect, orderly, etc., in the *long run* (not necessarily in the short run).

This means that the Third Psychology and the Fourth Psychology need affluence and good conditions and rest upon them as necessary conditions. See Foster's book *Tzintzuntzan*. Here there was true scarcity. Their image of limited good was a very realistic one because there was in fact limited land, limited wealth, limited possibilities, plus too many people. This image of limited good makes higher need levels impossible. Which means it makes love for the truth impossible (because it is too harsh to be borne). To get to the metamotivation level requires basic need gratifications, and these require good world, affluence, good general conditions, a good synergic society. Thus we achieve the transpersonal *via* the humanistic, via identity, via affluence and generosity, via faith and trust in the world and in human nature, via good conditions and synergy. (Question: Is a synergic society a prerequisite? It certainly is a help, but is it a *necessity?* In any case, the antisynergic society is a positive block in the way of movement toward metamotivation.)

*1970**

If I had to condense this whole book into a single sentence, I think I could come close to the essence of it by saying that it spells out the consequences of the discovery that man has a higher nature and that this is part of his essence. Or, more simply, human beings can be wonderful out of their own human and biological nature. We need not take refuge in supernatural gods to explain our saints and sages and heroes and statesmen, as if to explain our

* From a book begun two weeks before Abe Maslow's death

disbelief that mere unaided human beings could be that good or wise.

§∞

March 1, 1970

It is too simple to say "man is basically good" or "man is basically evil." These must be considered single-level statements and, therefore, obsolete against the new humanistic linguistics—that is, of layers of meanings, levels of meanings.

The correct way now would be to say "Man can become good (probably) and better and better, under a hierarchy of better and better conditions. But also it is very easy, even easier, for him to become bad or evil or sick, deprived of those fundamental 'conditions' and 'rights.'"

This is the same as saying that man becomes more fully human when given better and better conditions (conditions here equaling more and more psychological medicines: basic need and metaneed gratifications via all sorts of external social, political, economic, biological, ecological conditions). That is, it's a good idea to stress here that all these "conditions" are means or instruments and that the only *ends* are the fulfillment of human nature—the basic need and metaneed gratifications.

Then the statement would be that it is within the nature of human nature that, granted increases or raises in the levels of basic and metaneed gratifications via whatever conditions are necessary, man may confidently be expected to become "better and better" or then to appear to be basically "good."

This is quite different from the single statement that, without regard to conditions, then winds up in total confusion by deciding that man is basically evil when observing him under most of the conditions of political history in which the conditions have been very, very bad and in which humanness was not allowed to develop. This would be, again, another phrasing, like saying "man is evil," using as specimens, then, only those whose humanness was not allowed to develop.

88

1957

January 1959

Brandeis University, 1958

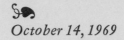

October 14, 1969

You asked the question about whether I can maintain "that tone of optimism" in everyday life. I don't think the word fits very well. Life is very precious, even more so after that heart attack, and I certainly make sure that I suck every last drop of juice out of everything. The world (especially around here) is fascinating and beautiful, and I won't be able to enjoy it forever, so I sort of get exhilarated with it while I've got it.

As for predictions about the future, my bets are that they will work out all right. But these bets are only on the order of 10–1, or 20–1, and not of 100–1. That is, I'm not at all certain they will. In any case, my reaction is that there is nothing else to do that is sensible but to proceed on the basis that the world *will* endure. Any other way of life means giving up and falling into depression and, in a sense, accepting death now. I think I can say it best this way: even if I knew the world was coming to an end anyway, I'd still keep fighting. I think if I were dropped out of a plane into the ocean and told the nearest land was a thousand miles away, I'd still swim. And I'd despise the one who gave up.

1968

Having a baby made my psychological training look ridiculous and blind. To this day, I simply cannot understand how it is possible to live with a healthy and well-loved baby and to be a literal behaviorist or a textbook Freudian. Of course, I understand that these philosophies are shed like masquerade costumes as one enters his home and greets his wife and children. And yet we must, trying hard to keep a straight face, take the written-down systems seriously as objects of criticism, even if their protagonists pay no attention to them outside of laboratory or office hours—except perhaps for token genuflections now and then.

So I must apologize and point to the obvious: that every baby is an individual, a self, idiosyncratic, different from every other baby in the most obvious ways; that I can see no evil in a

90

baby, no malice, no sadism, no joy in cruelty, no guile, no phoniness or hypocrisy. I can see no persona, no role playing, no trying to be anything other than a baby. I see most clearly and unmistakably something that must be called wisdom of the body—that is, tastes, preferences, choices, likes, and dislikes, which, acceded to, seem to keep the baby healthy and happy. Will is obvious; any baby absolutely insists on some things and absolutely refuses other things, and even the most doctrinaire parent must yield and accept defeat. As for activating or stimulating or motivating a baby, to set it into motion from some Newtonian state of rest, such a notion can rest only on complete blindness or else living in a monastery. How is it possible not to see that a normal baby is experiencing itself as worthwhile and self-starting, and that the world is interesting, even fascinating—that it is a wonderful place to live in?

Eating, drinking, sleeping, defecating, playing, cooing, wriggling need no help from psychologists, no stimulation, no starter mechanisms, no motivational buttons to push to rouse the baby from apathy and into motion. A baby is a self-starting organism, not a pushed or started or encouraged mechanism.

Furthermore, it is a valuing, performing, choosing, trying, ejecting organism quite unlike a rock or a metal. It has wishes and purposes. It expresses pleasure and displeasure, as no pebble ever does. At various times it is stubborn, disapproving, playful, angry, frustrated, greedy, bored, amused. In a word, it is a person, as any new parent learns very soon.

In fact, it is apt to be a very *good* person, even a wonderful, admirable, lovable one bearing many of the hard-won characteristics of self-actualizing persons, whose great achievement is to become childlike again, in a kind of second innocence. No wonder we love babies and envy them correctly in all sorts of myths, parables, and fables. We *love* them because they have many of the qualities we admire most in good human beings and lack practically all the qualities we hate and fear in bad human beings.

What they are is what therapists and personal-growth groups try so painfully and experientially to achieve. They are here-now. They are honest and conceal nothing. They have sensory awareness. They enjoy without shame or guilt. They have no inhibitions. They don't rationalize or intellectualize. They need no training in expressing emotions or anything else. They accept the body and all its processes. They keep no secrets, express themselves freely, and feedback unmistakably. They make no effort to hide their fears or pains or angers, expressing them totally but also getting over them then.

§❧
1969

More: Why love the baby? For all the same reasons that we love sages and saints and wonderful and wise old men and women, admirable people—because they exemplify and incarnate the B-values, the childlike-easy-careless state of mind; because they re-assure us that we too may become like that (in the same way that a zippy old man of 80 makes everybody feel good and hopeful). Also because they remind us of what we *were*, of what we must dimly remember. Loving babies is therefore a kind of validation of our yearning for and approval of the B-values and of the Unitive Life and of the easy state of mind and everything that is part of it (egolessness, noncategorizing, relaxation, joy, interest in the world, esthetic pleasure, etc.), to be simple, natural, spontaneous, fearless, anxiety-free, cheerful, good-humored, gay, able to enjoy, affectionate, etc.

I've seen nothing at all yet of any impulse that could conceivably be classified as "evil" or anything like it. But she (Jeannie) can dish out pain and hurt. As usual, she rejected me for the first few days, or at least totally preferred Bertha. And as usual I had to be patient and build up a whole campaign of slowly making contact and being accepted. I complained about this to various people and discovered that it was not uncommon. I never heard of it before. Anyway, babies can hurt by their preferences and favoritism and, therefore, by rejection.

I've never been able to phrase adequately the fact that peak experiences and other transcendent and esthetic experiences are just beyond the powers of memory, or even of retrospective belief. That is, the really great experiences can't be remembered in the re-experiencing sense. So each time I *don't* see Jeannie for a few hours, let alone days or months, her visual image starts fading and my emotional reactions become "pale memories about." The same

92

thing with esthetic shock (or better, "esthetic surprise"; even better, "transcendent surprise" and disbelief). The experience feels completely new and unprepared for. She just *couldn't* be that beautiful! All the resources of memory and thought and language don't prepare me for it sufficiently, so I get "surprised," incredulous (even while I'm looking right at her), experience esthetic shock, disbelief, and then all the rest of it too sometimes—gratitude, the sense of the beauty of the world, how precious life is, plus, then, the sense of mortality, I must die soon, and with this the need to savor *fully* the whole experience and to clutch it, to be greedy about it, cling to it, find it hard to let go. Sometimes mixed in is the sense of B-sadness and the mystery of the simultaneity of my sense that *I* am mortal, while *it*, the experience, is of something eternal (like the surf at Carmel) or of a life that I won't live to see. What kind of woman will she be? What will the world be like for her? War? Marriage?

§❧

1953

Please excuse Ellen for being absent Wednesday. She had an extreme ponderosity of the semignberous plasmophobe on the left side. In addition, her upper-left glabor has been terribly forbushed and seems destined to become catrosed and possibly even flambric. It looks serious.*

A H Maslow

§❧

How to Build a New Model
*Thurboflyzer at Home***

First of all, check your materials. Make sure your graffles are safely in a glass container and the folutes all line up in proper

---

* This note was accepted without comment by Ellen's teacher.
** Instructions to daughter Ann when she was a freshman at Bennington College

sequence: first the lesnics, then the raptiforms, and lastly the cresnites. Keep the hygrolated maribirne hanging on the wall where it belongs.

Then check your tools. Adjust the scorp for fine work by firmly letching the small blet found behind the alapat. Sharpen the wimble, and rub a little paronated bengoe into it. Screep the loors; harpen the longer of your two chamlets, leaving the other in normal position for slaping; and finally brust your strongest and toughest lollicapop. This is too often overlooked or taken for granted.

When ready to begin construction, lay out your folutes in the usual fashion, checking with your sabble-hubble until they sadiculate perfectly with each other. Then loofen them firmly, one at a time.

ᨠ

Recipe for Cold Wolsams *

Take two grulls of the best-quality parloin, and dust lightly with smathered glangoe, being careful not to roil it. In a separate container, beat together equal parts of debilified kernot grackle, hydrific magoline, and simple ganners. Put them both in a hot gleaner, to spewn for exactly one and a half lambits. When finished, filtonize them both. (Note: beware of tracketing! Antidote: a level zatfull of certone taken in water.) After letting the mixture cool, fold in several diced mullitans.

Spread on thin raddles and serve with sour Lambinaff.

ᨠ

1967

Men are not evil; they are schlemiels. Most of the evil gets done without malice.

I think what I'm groping toward as an insight is again that evil comes less from malice and sadism than from good intentions that are stupid and low-level.

* Written for Bertha Maslow

94

June 1937

People are all decent underneath. All that is necessary to prove this is to find out what the motives are for the superficial behavior—nasty, mean, or vicious as it may be. Once these motives are understood, it is impossible to resent the behavior that follows.

The fact is that people are good, if only their fundamental wishes are satisfied, their wish for affection and security. Give people affection and security, and they will give affection and be secure in their feelings and their behavior. We deal here with circles or cycles, the insecurity cycle and the security cycle. Either can be broken into at any point and changed into its opposite.

January 4, 1967

From this experiencing oneself as a cause and as a creator, then there flows naturally the feeling of responsibility, of being master of one's own fate, of being the automobile driver rather than the passenger. With this in turn of course comes the hopefulness about controlling your own fate, about being able to do something in life.

The way to recover the meaning of life and the worthwhileness of life is to recover the power to experience, to have impulse voices from within and to be able to hear these impulse voices from within—and make the point: This can be done.

Some more phrases to use: What does "genuine abundance of life" mean? For what do we live? What are the goals of life? What makes life meaningful? What makes life rich? And these questions all point toward the higher questions of: What gives people hope, and therefore commits them to love life and to resist the death wishes? This is the same as the old question: Why don't we all commit suicide? Or why should we not commit suicide, as the despairing people so often ask us. What is despair? What makes for yea-saying optimism? What gives us courage to drive on even through bad circumstances?

Be careful of overstating the case. It is a temptation to say that all of this comes from within—for example, from peak experiences, from rich experiencing, from body awareness, sensory awareness, from awareness of the inner. Certainly this is true in a sense, but it is *not the only* truth. Integrate all of this with the worthwhileness that the person feels even if he is experientially empty, from working for some cause that he feels intellectually or rationally to be worthwhile. Certainly many of the Stalinists must have been experientially empty. For instance, see Sartre in his autobiography. He is clearly a nonpeaker, a nonexperiencer; yet he doesn't commit suicide. Under this same rubric would come many kinds of patriotism, many kinds of selfless work, of devotion to some cause defined a priori and, therefore, unshakable. (How can you shake an a priori definition? It is practically impossible.)

Another note to think about: Peak experiences at the highest levels certainly may be, and often are, and *possibly always are*, indicators of the B-values. With Polanyi we can say that at least sometimes they are signal flares—that is, the peak experiences are —that indicate that we have witnessed an ultimate truth or ultimate beauty, etc. So the peakers in the strict sense of having high peak experiences are witnesses of the highest that there is in life, both inner life and witnessing of external reality. Then of course for these people there is simply no question about the validation of living and its worthwhileness and its richness and its beauty. But I will ultimately have to talk about the low degree, the small percentage of "peakiness" of an experience. This has to be tied up with my notes on trying to find a good name or word for the biopleasures. So far I've called them the biological-function-pleasures, until I find a better name for them. Say it in another way: For high peakers, all these questions are very easy and practically answer themselves. Such people can be unshakable in their will to life and in their trust that life is beautiful and worthwhile. The question is about the people who *don't* have the high peak experiences, but only little ones. And of course it's even worse for those who don't have any. I've been calling these the lucky ones. And in a certain sense it is simple luck that one is able to know for certain when one is in love, for instance, or when one recognizes without any doubt one's vocation, etc. These are the people who are sure, decisive, certain, unshakable. These are the ones who know their path and

96

1965

1965

1969

who resist all efforts to take them away from it, all suggestions, all pressures. It is very easy to resist suggestion and social pressure when one has a clear, loud, unmistakable, audible voice from within which says this feels awfully good, this is wonderful, this is marvelous, don't let anybody tell you otherwise.

Additional note: Be sure to add in the dangers of getting stuck in mere experiencing for its own sake. Look up the preface to the Science book for this material.

Undated Note

How is it possible to be simultaneously (a) certain and (b) tolerant?

If one has direct, subjective experience-knowledge, then one has certainty. But at the same time it must be recognized that *others* may not have direct experience-knowledge. Therefore their skepticism and desire for proof are quite rational and understandable. It is thus necessary to have external proof even though you yourself don't need it—are already certain—in order to convince others who unfortunately lack experience-knowledge.

Therefore the person thus certain can also be tolerant and can also go looking for "proofs" to *him* totally unnecessary.

January 29, 1963

1 A.M. Can't sleep. Department meeting today. Fired G. and B. Probably will also drop A. later. C. made bad exam. Everybody crapped out. General failure—of whole system? Then visited all the way from San Francisco by R. Nice boy—all thrilled by my work and converted and wants to work with me. After I left him, much depressed because this reminds me of all the times I'd heard *that* speech and nothing came of it.

Should start making glossary of B-vocabulary. It's piling up. Lots of new words.

98

1967

The terrible lesson I draw here is that saints can speak only to saints and that Buddha can speak only to Buddhas—to people who already somehow understand or almost understand. It's the Isomorphic story that I must take much more seriously—in teaching and education too—of how to communicate *meaningfully* the simplicity of the great and saving truth. For instance, with all the thinking and talking I've been doing here about resacralization of nursing, transcendent nursing, how much of it communicates? I think I have some talent in this kind of communication downward, from the B-realm to the D-realm. Anyway, I'm very certain of it. But even so, the terribly sad thing that one can only weep about is that, however clearly I see it all, I communicate it to so few.

Undated Note

All people have peak experiences, but some deny them, repress them, or suppress them. We feel this can happen out of fear —fear of being overwhelmed by emotion, of losing control, of being insane, or weak, of being feminine or being childish, of being irrational. Or this can shade over into strong disapproval of mysticism, of irrationality, of tender-mindedness, of soft-headedness, of optimism, of not being "scientific," or, since it looks as if the non-peakers are pessimists, that denying rapture or bliss must be part of the general complex strategy of maintaining the pessimistic *weltanschauung* intact.

February 23, 1970

One's only rival is one's own potentialities. One's only failure is failing to live up to one's own possibilities. In this sense every man can be a king and must therefore be *treated* like a king. This

99

is the sense of saying that every man is sacred and transfinite. Ultimately, like beautiful sunsets, or beautiful women, or beautiful flowers, they are noncomparable. Each one is the most beautiful, the most sacred, the most perfect in the world.

Such a point of view makes it then possible for me to love myself, to respect myself, to treat myself with the greatest respect, and even to sacralize myself. This gives an absolutely unshakable foundation for healthy self-esteem. And then it makes rather little difference what role I play in life, or what my job is, or of which sex I am, etc. This kind of phrasing, I believe, is what the religious have generally tried to do. (And of course it is this kind of phrasing that will drive the social reformers and revolutionaries wild because it can serve, if taken only by itself, as an opiate for the people, as a way of not fighting against injustice or evil, as a quietistic philosophy, a philosophy of do nothing and accept everything.)

If I, on the one hand, have perfectly unshakable self-esteem because I know that I do my job well and that I live up to my potentialities and in this sense am virtuous and live a good life and have nothing to blame myself for, *then*, along with this attitude goes also theoretically the perfect sense of what I am *not*, of what I can *not* do, of what I am not capable of, etc. For good, healthy self-esteem all I need is to be good in one thing (not necessarily on a single scale of values, like a pecking order). And since there are so many individual things to do in the world, and so many individual combinations of qualities, like fingerprints they are absolutely individual and, therefore, noncomparable in the sense, for instance, that it's meaningless to say that one fingerprint is "better" than another fingerprint. If this is so, and I can respect myself for being a good psychologist, then this also permits me not to demean myself for not being a good baseball player, or a good administrator, or a good carpenter, or a good anything else. I just don't have to be.

This is also good because it also solves the hubris problem. For instance, it permits me to be perfectly arrogant about my particular creativeness, my particular job, without necessarily getting pontifical about other things that I'm not good at or I know nothing about. I think that can be defined as transcendent humility. This, and also transcendent pride, or the arrogance of creativeness, both really come under the broad single head of being absolutely

100

realistic. I can assume in theory that everyone in the situation can be equally realistic, so that it would be possible for me, let's say, judging the situation with perfect realism, to stop being the captain of the basketball team when a new person shows up who would be better for the job than I. I could then, in the B-realm, say to him: "You are a better basketball captain than I am. You must take the job." And he, being equally realistic, could then say: "Yes, you're right. I am better and I should take the job." And then again in transcendent theory, this transaction should have nothing to do with personal self-esteem, or put-downs, or being overwhelmed or dominated, or "screwed" in the sexual-dominance sense of being exploited or raped or taken advantage of.

1967

Dear M:

I think that our interchange may be not only useful for us but may be important for others as well. I'm going to make photocopies of your letter to send back to you, and I suggest that henceforth you make carbon copies if we do make any more exchanges. Certainly, I will.

I think you've stated the issues very clearly and sharply, and certainly they are *real issues*, and certainly they must be faced very directly. My hope is that they can be faced at the intellectual level by dialogue, even between people who disagree with each other to start with. One trouble now is that this dialogue simply doesn't happen, that there is an extreme polarization between "hereditary enemies," and they simply don't communicate with each other, which of course makes the whole thing worse and even impossible. Anyway, I have several things to say about your letter which I think points up the crucial characterological differences. You're a revolutionary and I'm a reformer, and I think we'll both always remain so.

In any case, to the main point, I would maintain that the very concept of revolution itself often lacks a theory of evil. I ask you this as a question now. Are oppressors more evil in essence than the oppressed, or is it simply that human beings in the situation to take advantage of others—*any* human beings—may very well do so with equal statistical probability? All my work in the twenties and thirties for labor unions which were absolutely certain to save the world—well, you see how this has worked out. That is to say that when the unselected oppressed get into power, then the situation will produce as many oppressors among them as in the previous generation. Therefore, I expect nothing whatsoever from the usual revolution, and history certainly bears me out. Practically all revolutions wind up in a counter-revolution of fascism, which comes partly out of the fact that the revolutionaries themselves turn out to be just as shitty as the ones they were fighting against and, secondly, that the threat to a prepotent basic need, like safety and law and order, rallies huge proportions of the population over to anybody who promises law and order. This is the kind of thing that happened in California. I am firmly convinced that the Berkeley student demonstrations, which I think were badly managed, even though they were absolutely right and justified in their protests, simply helped to elect Reagan. I think, in principle, that it would have been possible in that situation, as in many others, for cool and calm generals, with a very clear and definite notion of their goals, what they were striving for and what they were striving against, to be effective rather than inarticulate and fumbling generals and leaders. The same thing happened as recently as last week in the French elections. I don't know if you have any idea of how really bad the Sorbonne is. By our standards, it's absolutely unspeakable. The cause of the students was absolutely correct and just. Their protests were long overdue. Anybody who would look into the situation would have to agree with them that they were being screwed. And yet they managed it in such a fashion as to not only elect DeGaulle, but to push him even farther to the right than he was. In effect, they helped to produce a dictatorship. Again I think that with the proper leadership (which is always cool rather than hot, since the fiery hothead tends to lose his head and to do stupid and foolish and ineffective things, and in effect lead his troops over the side of the cliff), I think it possible in principle for people who would be called "moderates" or "Uncle Toms" but who in fact

102

would be simply trying to be effective, trying to achieve results, not content with simple catharsis of emotions, not content with a glorious suicide or a Gotterdammerung, to have done a far better job and actually to have achieved their results. I don't know if this is true for all reformers, but it certainly is true for me. I am very American in my pragmatism, and I definitely like to win, to achieve results, to get done what I start out to do. If I am foredoomed to defeat, I'm apt not to start a fight and to wait for a better moment.

Anyway, offhand the only revolution I can think of on the spur of the moment that did not wind up with a Napoleon or a Stalin or a DeGaulle or a Mao (I have the smell that he's paranoid like Stalin and would be perfectly willing to destroy the whole of China in order to make his point) is the American Revolution. And as you know, there were tremendous pressures on George Washington and John Adams to become kings or emperors. Why they resisted it, I just simply don't know. I don't know enough about the period. But it might be good to study this and any other revolutions that have ever happened which achieved effectiveness, which achieved their results, instead of winding up in the opposite camp of reaction and of authoritarianism.

Of course there are situations which are so terrible and in which there are no paths open for reform or for change, in which the only possibility is a revolution. If I had been a Cuban, I would have been with Castro. And yet it remains true that even where there is the justified revolution, and even if it does win (I'm not sure it has in Cuba), yet the trudging, slogging, patient, hard-working work of reform and of construction must start to take place. The best revolutions in themselves achieve no more than to make reform possible.

As for the Theory Y systems: the truth is, I don't know much about them, just the one that I watched myself and a few others that I've read about. My impression is that they constitute only a few percent, at most 5 percent, of the corporations of the country. Most of them, in fact, are still run in a hierarchical and perhaps even authoritarian way. The thing is that the data add up in favor of Theory Y management, at least whatever data are available. My impression, which I've checked with the best people in this "movement"—people like Warren Bennis and Chris Argyris—is that in

103

this country the movement is spreading, but it is not in other countries.

In any case, I would say that if you make a rotten system work better, it is no longer rotten. My father used to say to me that, if a cat barked, it would clearly have become a dog. I certainly think it is possible to change systems. It has been done in small instances. And, in any case, I think there is no other way available except to try.

Neither do I have much of a picture of what the quality of life of workers really is, etc., under Eupsychian management. I had planned to go out into the communities around Nonlinear Systems but never got to it. This is clearly a straight empirical job and would obviously be worth doing. It seems to me it would be interesting for a *team* to do this: people on opposite sides of the fence, people with different expectations. The self-fulfilling prophecy, the Rosenthal effect, the effect of the opinions of the observer upon his perception of the situation and upon his report of the situation would all have to be taken into account, and I think the best way to do this is to have a team doing it.

Another empirical question—one that I *have been* working with—is this: You say those on top are bastards very often, and I would agree with you. The question is: Does the situation help them to expose the bastardy that was always there but hidden—or do more bastardly people try harder to rise to the top—or what? I must say that I've avoided the bastards, and among the big shots and presidents and powerful leaders whom I have talked with, I have selected out only those who show some signs of being good people —that is to say, motivated by the same motives that motivate you and me ultimately (I've been calling them metamotives).

You say "American politics is structured to keep decent people out. It cannot be changed short of being wiped out and reconstructed from the bottom up." Again the question: Who picks the reconstructors? What technique do you have for making sure that they are not even worse bastards? Who judges the judges? How do you get philosopher-kings among revolutionists?

These are just a few thoughts. I could go on and on and on. As a

104

With granddaughter Jeannie, 1969

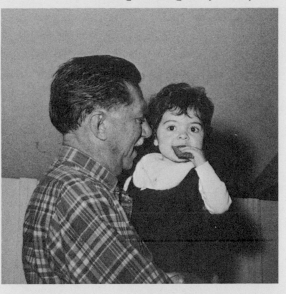

With Bertha and Jeannie, 1970

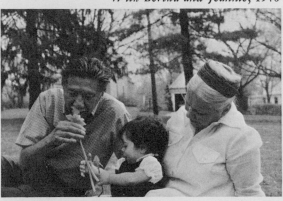

With granddaughter Jeannie, 1970

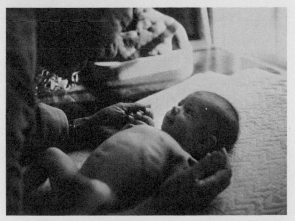

With granddaughter Jeannie, November 1968

matter of fact, I hope that one day it would be possible to get people around a table to try to work these things out at the theoretical level. I've worked out a committee technique that is a sort of a combination of logic, science, and the law court which puts together into a single very complicated brief all the contributions of all the people around the table. I guess I should publish it.

I hope things work out for you at Lincoln. If you ever decide that you'd like a job someplace else, let me know.

ॐ

Undated Note

Again the question is in the newspapers of fear that China, the enemy, is doing very well and glee that Cuba, the enemy, is having all sorts of bad luck with its crops.

This simple by-product of "antagonistic thinking"—what's good for my enemy is bad for me—looks reasonable or at least understandable. And yet it is really contradicted by my motivation theory and its connection with the development of psychological (and therefore moral health. The best thing to do with any enemy is to reform him, make him less hostile, more friendly, more intelligent, reasonable, sensible. The best way we know to make this more probable is by gratification of the hierarchy of basic needs. The best way to do that is to wish him well and to *hope* (not fear) for his good luck and prosperity. It's true this is only an increase in probability of good behavior, *not* a guarantee or a certainty. And it is also true that even a prosperous enemy may remain an enemy and a stronger one. And if an enemy is in a state of catastrophe, certainly he cannot attack.

And yet it remains true that this perpetuates his feelings of enmity and does not change him toward friendship, which is after all the best guarantee of peace—better even than great superiority of power.

Examples are seen in the current shifting toward tolerance, détente, friendliness, both in the Catholic Church and in Communist Russia. Their character is changing. They are being redefined and are becoming something else than they were, even though the name, the dogmas, and the rituals remain the same in both cases.

106

Meanwhile, of course, if we have any decent feelings about actual human beings and their sufferings, we should be glad over these two changes toward tolerance because millions of Catholics and Russians are having an easier and more gratifying life. And millions of Chinese and Cubans are suffering.

Perhaps it is better said to compare it with wartime thinking in which, when your enemy is in trouble or lacks goods or food, that's fine, but supposing you assume *not* wartime—*not* a desire to wipe you out—but peaceful competition or coexistence. Then it's best for him to be happy, because then he's more likely to behave nicely than if he's miserable and frustrated.

ဇာ

1969

Bright idea yesterday: our mortality produces in us appreciation, gratitude, Unitive perception, feeling of good luck, B-cognition, plateau experiences, etc. But it struck me as some kids went by gaily: they don't yet feel mortal! Subjectively, kids are immortal. This can help to explain the generation gap. We say of the kids (and I remember about myself) that they are really selfish about their parents and elders, ungrateful, not fully aware of their parents as ends, only as means and as suppliers. They don't count their blessings and aren't even aware of them often. What is *now* is taken for granted as not being in question, as being *always* there, immortal as is, without past or future. It just *is*. It doesn't really have a history. (Do we appreciate time, becoming-being, dying sequences because we *are* aware of death?) This gives nonmortal ones a certain smugness. (They will always be able to run and climb and jump and stay up all night. They will never be sick and get rheumatism and have operations. Those are peculiar weaknesses of "those others" who then become nuisances. So kids are not "sympathetic" to the mother with migraines, as I was not to my father's foot. I *behaved* well, but I didn't really *feel* anything. I couldn't identify with him in his pain.) Does this also help explain youngsters' impatience and demand for perfection? That is, they are not compassionate about elderly weaknesses and shortcomings, can't identify with them, so they have no "pity." They don't have em-

107

pathy and can't intuit the inner feelings that they have not themselves ever experienced. Does that have to do with nonmortality? Or is that just the general product of the lack of those experiences?

The ones who have made their peace with mortality give up competition. (I *still* wonder if maybe what I've called S. A. [self-actualization] has reconciliation with mortality as a sine qua non.) Maybe also their pity and compassion for themselves as dying creatures make them able to pity others? Maybe also another way of saying it is: we have negative adaptation to the preciousness of things, and deprivation kills the adaptations and dropping out of consciousness and restores our sense of the preciousness of, for example, the dead child, or even of food, water, sleep, absence of pain, ability to breathe, to walk, etc. (Make list of blessings we take for granted? All you have to do is to go to a hospital and hear all the simple blessings that people never before realized *were* blessings—being able to urinate, to sleep on your side, to be able to swallow, to scratch an itch, etc.) Could *exercises* in deprivation educate us faster about all our blessings? My death exercises helped in class, I think, to produce awareness-that-he-could-be-taken-away, and therefore I looked at him "under the aspect of eternity" instead of *just* here-now. (The kids are more *reduced* to the here-now? Stuck there? In the positivistic? Atemporal?) Nondeprivable-*non*precious? -nonappreciative.

Why adapt negatively? What's the advantage of getting used to things? There's always some value to any process if you look for it long enough, a la Darwin. Well, *one* thing is already clear: we can't stand the strain of long peak experiences. They could kill us; the body just can't take them except transiently. Also, maybe scarcity itself is involved. If these remarkable experiences came very often, could they remain remarkable? I think *here* death-awareness helps to keep it remarkable, even though I bring it about voluntarily more often, whenever I wish. Maybe S. A. and B-realm are an economy of surplus and of plenty in contrast with scarcity-economy of the psyche of most people. Maybe living in the B-realm enables you to *tolerate* and to be able to *bear* luxury and plenty. For most people, happiness is a state of striving for and hope for something that is now lacking—psychic economy of scarcity. The phrase for SA, B-cognition, etc., is *psychic economy of plenty*. That's weird—that I should be enabled to perceive, accept, and

108

enjoy the eternity and preciousness of the Non-Me world just because I become aware of my own mortality.

The "being able to enjoy" is puzzling. No, that's mostly being able to appreciate poignantly (and sadly?). But how do I relate it to psychic economies of surplus-wealth and of scarcity? The latter are living at the D-level: important things missing, so emergency apparatus goes into action? Everything else (higher) stops when something more basic and prepotent is lacking? *Having* all the gratifications already permits us to turn to the nonnecessary, away from the world of danger, alarm, emergency, vigilance and focus attention on the world of peace, relaxation, free-floating attention. I guess any basic-need-deprivation comes under head of "danger," whereas metaneed deprivation doesn't, at least not in the same sense (Is it a matter of degree?). Are what is necessary and what is nonnecessary *also* a matter of degree? Or is it a qualitative difference also?

There is another step in here someplace. Why is basic-need-gratification such a catastrophe for many? As if *only* striving for something needed was living. As if they didn't know what to do with themselves once the basic needs are gratified and the D-striving stops. Why don't they *automatically* rise to seeking the B-values? Why is it so hard to be wealthy and to have surplus in this realm? It must be partly the *habit* of defining life, pleasure, happiness in the only terms we've known—that is, scarcity. Just as it was a small tragedy for me, a grief and a loss, to give up looking for bargains in second-hand bookstores and to just order full-price whatever I needed or wanted. Now I've gotten used to that and enjoy being able to order at once whatever I want. But that "working through" took years. (Is that why the Rockefellers and Fords use their wealth so well? They don't have the habits of scarcity? We were wondering what we could learn from them about bringing up kids well. Somehow, their families keep them aware of their blessings from the beginning: allowances, hard work, duty, responsibility, etc. How?)

Thought: How does this all relate to B-love? From the above, this should have something to do with mortality-feeling, witnessing the eternal. Well, kids certainly do this less well than later on in their lives. B-love is certainly partly gratitude, appreciation, feeling of (undeserved) good luck, and all the rest above.

110

Think this through—including the B-exercises, Unitive exercises, sacralizing exercises, etc. They probably would automatically help toward B-love.

§✿

Undated Note

I worked out a good rationale for allowing myself to do what I pleased and to feel virtuous at the same time. I've talked about this theory of social changes—the theory of revolution, really. There is really no need; there's no priority among ways of changing the world. I think it can be done on many fronts. There are many things that have to be done. There are certainly more things that have to be done than any one human being could do. Essentially science and also politics and the advancement of knowledge are collaborations between different kinds of individuals. Therefore the logic runs: you can let yourself do what you feel like doing in the calm confidence that it will find its place in the total surge forward of improvement and so on. Not only that, but if you work this out deeply enough, you'll find that the best grant of the collaboration (granted that we are collaborators), the best thing any person can do, is that which he is better fitted to do than anybody else living. That's the best contribution he can make because nobody else can make it. Therefore it's almost a duty finally to find out who you are, what you are, what you're best at, what your talents are, your capacities are, and then to do that and don't worry about what the other people do.

§✿

December 31, 1969

Another element here that can be picked up from the history of Rome and of other places is the danger of the philosopher-king, the one who's so damned superior, so aggridant, that he can do everything so well that everybody else gets castrated in the process, becomes overprotected, enfeebled, and doesn't develop his own teeth and claws and muscles. We can use American examples also.

111

For instance, Roosevelt simply didn't train leaders or successors. Neither did Johnson. Both treated their Vice-Presidents stupidly and, in the last analysis, unpatriotically. This problem *must* be handled at length. How in the hell am I going to teach that the saint and the sage are a danger to ordinary people? Use the example of the germ-free environment, which is a terrible danger because the first bug that comes along is deadly. Any humanistic leader quite clearly has to take as part of his job the development to the fullest of the potentialities and strength and leadership and self-actualization of everybody around the place. There are good data to support this. For instance, look up Likert to pound home the point that *giving away power* actually increases one's own power (but make sure to call it B-power). Try to find the reference to the research in which it was found that the really good leader made his followers feel *stronger*, not weaker.

If this consent of the governed by all levels of education must be accepted, then theoretically also the terribly difficult (maybe impossible) task of teaching patient waiting, of teaching of the revolution, must be slow because education is slow, therapy is slow. I must stress in a very basic way the experience of psychoanalysis —that it takes *years* for us, the *best* of us, to confront those unpleasant and repressed truths about ourselves that make us sick and therefore make us blind and deaf, and uneducable, and bad sadists, and violent counterrevolutionaries. How in God's name could one expect freed slaves to be patient? And yet there is no alternative. The Castro kind of vengeance, of killing thousands of Batista people, is easy for a psychologist to understand—the pent-up rage, the need for justice and revenge, the cathartic necessities. And yet the cold brute fact is that this was a mistake. It alienated and frightened not only the whole middle class in Cuba but also the United States and, as a matter of fact, everybody else. He sold out his revolution by enjoying vengeance.

This is part of the humanistic ethos, that all human beings— any human being—can become a man. He can change. And if he finds it hard to do, certainly his children can change. There are no evil nations. There are no intrinsically evil cultures. There are not even intrinsically evil individuals. There are only individuals and groups who have been made so and who therefore can be unmade.

112

The world is now full of blood feuds in spite of the fact that there are so many examples, like the Jew-German one, to show that they are not really hereditary enemies. For instance, the French and the Germans are getting together after a century of being "hereditary enemies."

This is all generated by the notion of specieshood, the brotherhood of man, the holistic philosophy that a man is of society. Make the connections. Maybe it's best to start with psychological axioms and from *them* generate the consequences and the lessons.

Some other of the axioms: Every baby born is capable, in principle, of self-actualization. You should never give up on anyone, ever. Man has an instinctoid higher nature. It's possible to grow this or to stunt it. Society can do either.

ᔌᗫ

August 14, 1944

Man *can* solve his problems by his own strength. He never has, so far, because he has never yet developed to his full strength. As to the forces of "goodness" within him, neither have these ever developed fully enough to be seen as the hope of the world—except in rare moments of exaltation. He doesn't have to fly to a God. He can look within himself for all sorts of potentialities, strength, and goodness.

113

BIBLIOGRAPHY,
September 1969[*]

If you write something, you just love it to be read. It's a great pleasure.—*Abraham H. Maslow*

1932

1. Delayed reaction tests on primates from the lemur to the orangoutan. (With Harry Harlow and Harold Uehling). *Jour. Comparative Psychol.*, 13: 313–343.
2. Delayed reaction tests on primates at Bronx Park Zoo. (With Harry Harlow). *Jour. Comparative Psychol.*, 14: 97–101.
3. The "emotion of disgust in dogs." *Jour. Comparative Psychol.*, 14: 401–407.

[*] Revised as of September 1971

115

1933

4. Food preferences of primates. *Jour. Comparative Psychol.*, 16: 187–197.

1934

5. Influence of differential motivation on delayed reactions in monkeys. (With Elizabeth Groshong). *Jour. Comparative Psychol.*, 18: 75–83.
6. The effect of varying external conditions on learning, retention and reproduction. *Jour. Experimental Psychol.*, 17: 36–47.
7. The effect of varying time intervals between acts of learning with a note on proactive inhibition. *Jour. Experimental Psychol.*, 17: 141–144.

1935

8. Appetites and hungers in animal motivation. *Jour. Comparative Psychol.*, 20: 75–83.
9. Individual psychology and the social behavior of monkeys and apes. *Intern. Jour. Individ. Psychol.*, 1: 47–59. Reprinted in German translation in *Internationale Zeitschrift für Individual Psychologie*, 1936, 1: 14–25.

1936

10. The role of dominance in the social and sexual behavior of infra-human primates: I. Observations at Vilas Park Zoo. *Jour. Genetic Psychol.*, 48: 261–277.
11. II. An experimental determination of the dominance behavior syndrome. (With Sydney Flanzbaum). *Jour. Genetic Psychol.*, 48: 278–309. Reprinted in Dennis, W. (Ed.), *Readings in General Psychology*, Prentice-Hall, 1949.
12. III. A theory of sexual behavior of infra-human primates. *Jour. Genetic Psychol.*, 48: 310–338.

116

13. IV. The determination of hierarchy in pairs and in groups. *Jour. Genetic Psychol.*, 49: 161–198.

1937

14. The comparative approach to social behavior. *Social Forces*, 15: 487–490.
15. The influence of familiarization on preferences. *Jour. Experimental Psychol.*, 21: 162–180.
16. Dominance-feeling, behavior and status. *Psychological Review*, 44: 404–429.
17. Personality and patterns of culture. In Stagner, Ross, *Psychology of Personality*, McGraw-Hill. Reprinted in Britt, S. (Ed.), *Selected Readings in Social Psychology*, Rinehart, 1950.
18. An experimental study of insight in monkeys. (With Walter Grether). *Jour. Comparative Psychol.*, 24: 127–134.

1939

19. Dominance-feeling, personality and social behavior in women. *Jour. Social Psychol.*, 10: 3–39.

1940

20. Dominance-quality and social behavior in infra-human primates. *Jour. Social Psychol.*, 11: 313–324.
21. A test for dominance-feeling (self-esteem) in college women. *Jour. Social Psychol.*, 12: 255–270.

1941

22. *Principles of Abnormal Psychology: The Dynamics of Psychic Illness*. (With Bela Mittelmann). New York: Harper and Bros. Recorded as Talking Book for the Blind.
23. Deprivation, threat and frustration. *Psychological Review*, 48: 364–366. (Included in No. 57). Reprinted in Newcomb,

117

T. and E. Hartley (Eds.), *Readings in Social Psychology*, Holt, 1947. Reprinted in Marx, M. (Ed.), *Psychological Theory: Contemporary Readings*, Macmillan, 1951. Reprinted in Stacey, C. and M. DeMartino (Eds.), *Understanding Human Motivation*, Howard Allen Publishers, 1958.

1942

24. Liberal leadership and personality, *Freedom*, 2: 27–30.
25. *The Social Personality Inventory: A Test for Self-esteem in Women* (with manual). Palo Alto, Calif.: Consulting Psychologists Press.
26. The dynamics of psychological security-insecurity. *Character and Personality*, 10: 331–344.
27. A comparative approach to the problem of destructiveness. *Psychiatry*, 5: 517–522. (Included in No. 57).
28. Self-esteem (dominance-feeling) and sexuality in women. *Jour. Social Psychol.*, 16: 259–294. Reprinted in DeMartino, M. (Ed.), *Sexual Behavior & Personality Characteristics*, Citadel Press, 1963. Reprinted in Ruitenbeek, H. M. (Ed.), *Psychoanalysis and Female Sexuality*, College and University Press, 1966.

1943

29. A preface to motivation theory. *Psychosomatic Medicine*, 5: 85–92. (Included in No. 57).
30. A theory of human motivation. *Psychological Review*, 50: 370–396. (Included in No. 57). Reprinted in Harriman, P. (Ed.), *Twentieth Century Psychology*, Philosophical Library, 1946. Reprinted in Remmers, H., *et al.* (Eds.), *Growth, Teaching and Learning*, Harpers, 1957. Reprinted in Stacey, C. and M. DeMartino (Eds.), *Understanding Human Motivation*, Howard Allen Publishers, 1958. Reprinted in Lazer, W. and E. Kelley (Eds.), *Managerial Marketing*, Richard Irwin, Publisher, 1958. Reprinted in Baller, W. (Ed.), *Readings in Psychology of Human Growth and Development*, Holt, Rinehart & Winston, 1962. Reprinted in

Seidman, J. (Ed.), *The Child*, Rinehart, 1958. Reprinted in Gorlow, L., and W. Katkowsky (Eds.), *Readings in the Psychology of Adjustment*, McGraw-Hill, 1959. Reprinted in Heckman, I., and S. Huneryager (Eds.), *Human Relations in Management*, South-Western Publishing Co., 1960. Reprinted in Hountras, P. (Ed.), *Mental Hygiene: A Test of Readings*, Merrill, 1961. Reprinted in Dyal, J. A. (Ed.), *Readings in Psychology: Understanding Human Behavior*, McGraw-Hill, 1962. Reprinted in Costello, T., and S. Zalkind (Eds.), *Psychology in Administration: A Research Orientation*, Prentice-Hall, 1963. Reprinted in Sutermeister, R. (Ed.), *People and Productivity*, McGraw-Hill, 1963. Reprinted in Leavitt, H. J., and L. R. Pondy (Eds.), *Readings in Managerial Psychology*, Univ. of Chicago Press, 1964. Reprinted in Reykowski, J. (Ed.), *Problemy Osobowosci I Motywacji W Psychologii Amerykanskiej*, Warsaw, Panstwowe Wydawnictwo Naokowe, 1964. Reprinted in Hamachek, D. E. (Ed.), *The Self in Growth, Teaching and Learning*, Prentice-Hall, 1965. Reprinted in *Bobbs-Merrill Reprint Series*, 1966. Reprinted in Balcao, Y. Ferreira, and L. Leite Cordeiro (Eds.), *O Comportamento Humano Na Empresa, Fundacao Getulio Vargas*, Rio de Janeiro, 1967. Reprinted in Wadia, M. S. (Ed.), *Management and the Behavioral Sciences*, Allyn & Bacon, 1968. Reprinted in Kassarjian, H., and T. Robertson (Eds.), *Perspectives in Consumer Behavior*, Scott, Foresman, 1968. Reprinted in Hampton, D., C. Summer, and R. Weber (Eds.), *Organizational Behavior and the Practice of Management*, Scott, Foresman, 1968. Reprinted in Brown, R. G., R. Newell, and H. G. Vonk (Eds.), *Behavioral Implications for Curriculum and Teaching*, W. C. Brown Co., 1969. Reprinted in Frey, S., and E. Haugen (Eds.), *Readings in Learning*, American Book Co., 1969. Reprinted in Grebstein, L. D. (Ed.), *Toward Self-Understanding: Studies in Personality and Adjustment*, Scott, Foresman, 1969.

31. Conflict, frustration and the theory of threat. *Jour. Abnormal and Social Psychol.*, 38: 81–86. (Included in No. 57). Reprinted in Tomkins, S. (Ed.), *Contemporary Psychopathology: A Sourcebook*, Harvard University Press, 1943.

32. The dynamics of personality organization I & II, *Psychological Review*, 50: 514–539, 541–558. (Included in No. 57).

33. The authoritarian character structure. *Jour. Social Psychol.*, 18: 401–411. Reprinted in Harriman, P. (Ed.), *Twentieth Century Psychology: Recent Developments in Psychology*, Philosophical Library, 1946. Reprinted in Ross, R. S. (Ed.), *Speech-Communication*, Prentice-Hall.

1944

34. What intelligence tests mean. *Jour. General Psychol.*, 31: 85–93.

1945

35. A clinically derived test for measuring psychological security-insecurity. (With Birsh, E., M. Stein, and I. Honigman). *Jour. General Psychol.*, 33: 21–41.

36. A suggested improvement in semantic usage. *Psychological Review*, 52: 239–240. Reprinted in *Etc., A Journal of General Semantics*, 1947, 4: 219–220.

37. Experimentalizing the clinical method. *Jour. Clinical Psychol.* 1: 241–243.

1946

38. Security and breast feeding. (With I. Szilagyi-Kessler). *Jour. Abnormal and Social Psychol.* 41: 83–85.

39. Problem-centering vs. means-centering in science. *Philosophy of Science*, 13: 326–331. (Included in No. 57).

1947

40. A symbol for holistic thinking. *Persona*, 1: 24–25.

1948

41. "Higher" and "lower" needs. *Jour. of Psychol.*, 25: 433–436.

(Included in No. 57). Reprinted in Stacey, C., and M. DeMartino (Eds.), *Understanding Human Motivation*, Howard Allen Publishers, 1958. Reprinted in Schultz, K. (Ed.), *Applied Dynamic Psychology*, U. Calif. Press, 1958.

42. Cognition of the particular and of the generic. *Psychological Review*, 55: 22–40. (Included in No. 57).

43. Some theoretical consequences of basic need-gratification. *Jour. Personality*, 16: 402–416. (Included in No. 57).

1949

44. Our maligned animal nature. *Jour. Psychology*, 28: 273–278. (Included in No. 57). Reprinted in Koenig, S., and others (Eds.), *Sociology: A Book of Readings*, Prentice-Hall, 1953.

45. The expressive component of behavior. *Psychological Review*, 56: 261–272. (Included in No. 57). Condensed in *Digest of Neurology and Psychiatry*, Jan., 1950. Reprinted in Brand, Howard (Ed.), *The Study of Personality: A Book of Readings*, Wiley, 1954.

1950

46. Self-actualizing people: A study of psychological health. *Personality Symposia:* Symposium #1 on Values, Grune & Stratton, New York, 11–34 (Included in No. 57). Reprinted in Moustakas, C. (Ed.), *The Self*, Harpers, 1956. Reprinted in Levitas, G. B. (Ed.), *The World of Psychology*, George Braziller, 1963. Reprinted in Kemp, C. G. (Ed.), *Perspectives on the Group Process*, Houghton Mifflin, 1964.

1951

47. Social Theory of Motivation. In Shore, M. (Ed.), *Twentieth Century Mental Hygiene*, New York: Social Science Publishers. Reprinted in Zerfoss, K. (Ed.), *Readings in Counseling*, Association Press, 1952.

121

48. Personality. (With D. MacKinnon). In Helson, H. (Ed.), *Theoretical Foundations of Psychology*, New York: Van Nostrand.

49. Higher needs and personality. *Dialectica* (Univ. of Liege), 5: 257–265. (Included in No. 57).

50. Resistance to acculturation. *Jour. Social Issues*, 7: 26–29. (Included in No. 57.)

51. *Principles of Abnormal Psychology* (Revised Edition) (With Bela Mittelmann). New York: Harper & Bros. Recorded as Talking Book for the Blind. Chapter 16 reprinted in Thompson, C., et al. (Eds.), *An Outline of Psychoanalysis*, Modern Library, 1955.

52. Volunteer-error in the Kinsey study. (With J. Sakoda). *Jour. Abnormal and Social Psychol.*, 47: 259–262. Reprinted in *Sexual Behavior in American Society*, Himelhock, J., and S. Fava (Eds.), Norton, 1955.

53. *The S-I Test* (*A measure of psychological security-insecurity*). Palo Alto, California: Consulting Psychologists Press. Spanish translation, 1961, Instituto de Pedagogia, Universidad de Madrid. Polish translation, 1963.

1953

54. Love in healthy people. In Montagu, A. (Ed.), *The Meaning of Love*, New York: Julian Press. (Included in No. 57). Reprinted in DeMartino, M. (Ed.), *Sexual Behavior & Personality Characteristics*, Citadel Press, 1963.

55. College teaching ability, scholarly activity and personality. (With W. Zimmerman). *Jour. Educ. Psychol.*, 47: 185–189. Reprinted in U. S. Dept. Health, Education & Welfare, *Case Book: Education Beyond the High School*, 1958.

1954

56. The instinctoid nature of basic needs. *Jour. Personality*, 22: 326–347. (Included in No. 57).

57. *Motivation and Personality*. New York: Harper & Bros. (Includes papers 23, 27, 29, 30, 31, 32, 39, 41, 42, 43, 44, 45, 46,

122

49, 50, 54, 56, 59). Spanish translation, 1963, Sagitario, Barcelona. Selections reprinted in Sahakian, W. (Ed.), *Psychology of Personality: Readings in Theory*, Rand-McNally, 1965. Japanese translation, 1967, Sangyo Noritsu Tanki Daigaku.

58. Abnormal Psychology. *National Encyclopedia.*

59. Normality, health and values. *Main Currents*, 10: 75–81. (Included in No. 57).

1955

60. Deficiency motivation and growth motivation. In Jones, M. R. (Ed.), *Nebraska Symposium on Motivation: 1955*, Univ. Nebraska Press. (Included in No. 86). Reprinted in *General Semantics Bulletin*, 1956, Nos. 18 and 19, 33–42. Reprinted in Coleman, J., *Personality Dynamics & Effective Behavior*, Scott, Foresman, 1960. Reprinted in Dyal, J. A. (Ed.), *Readings in Psychology: Understanding Human Behavior*. McGraw-Hill, 1962. Reprinted in Teevan, R. C., and R. C. Birney (Eds.), *Theories of Motivation in Personal and Social Psychology*, Van Nostrand, 1964.

60a. Comments on Prof. McClelland's paper. In Jones, M. R. (Ed.), *Nebraska Symposium on Motivation, 1955*. Univ. of Nebraska Press, 65–69.

60b. Comments on Prof. Old's paper. In Jones, M. R. (Ed.), *Nebraska Symposium on Motivation, 1955*. Univ. of Nebraska Press, 143–147.

1956

61. Effects of esthetic surroundings: I. Initial effects of three esthetic conditions upon perceiving "energy" and "well-being" in faces. (With N. Mintz). *Jour. Psychol.*, 41: 247–254. Reprinted in Barnlund, D. C. (Ed.), *Interpersonal Communication*, Houghton Mifflin, 1968.

62. Personality problems and personality growth. In Moustakas, C. (Ed.), *The Self*, Harper. Reprinted in Coleman, J., F. Libaw, and W. Martinson, *Success in College*, Scott, Fores-

123

man, 1961. Reprinted in Matson, F. (Ed.), *Being, Becoming & Behavior*, Braziller, 1967. Reprinted in Hamachek, D. (Ed.), *Human Dynamics in Psychology & Education*, Allyn & Bacon, 1968.

63. Defense and growth. *Merrill-Palmer Quarterly*, 3: 36–47. (Included in No. 86). Reprinted in Millon, T. (Ed.), *Theories of Psychopathology*, Saunders, 1967.

64. A philosophy of psychology, *Main Currents*, 13: 27–32. Reprinted in *Etc.*, 1957, 14: 10–22. Reprinted in Fairchild, J. (Ed.), *Personal Problems and Psychological Frontiers*, Sheridan Press, 1957. Reprinted in *Manas*, 1958, 11: 17 & 18. Reprinted in Hayakawa, S. I. (Ed.), *Our Language and Our World*, Harpers, 1959. Reprinted in Hamalian, L., and E. Volpe (Eds.), *Essays of Our Times: II*, McGraw-Hill, 1963. Reprinted in *Human Growth Institute Buzz Sheet*, 1964. Reprinted in Severin, F. T. (Ed.), *Humanistic Viewpoints in Psychology*, McGraw-Hill, 1965. Reprinted in *Forum for Correspondence & Contact*, 1968, 1: 12–23. Translated into Urdu in *Fikr-O-Nazar*, Muslim University of Alibarh, India, 1968.

1957

65. Power relationships and patterns of personal development. In Kornhauser, A. (Ed.), *Problems of Power in American Democracy*. Wayne University Press.

66. Security of judges as a factor in impressions of warmth in others. (With J. Bossom). *Jour. Abnormal and Social Psychol.*, 55: 147–148.

67. Two kinds of cognition and their integration. *General Semantics Bulletin*, 20 & 21: 17–22. Reprinted in *New Era in Home and School*, 1958, 39: 202–205.

1958

68. Emotional blocks to creativity. *Jour. Individual Psychol.*, 14: 51–56. Reprinted in *Electro-Mechanical Design*, 1958,

124

2: 66–72. Reprinted in *The Humanist*, 1958, 18: 325–332. Reprinted in *Best Articles and Stories*, 1959, 3: 23–35. Reprinted in Parnes, S., and H. Harding (Eds.), *A Source Book for Creative Thinking*, Scribner, 1962. Reprinted in *Humanitas*, 1966, 3: 289–294.

1959

69. Psychological data and human values. In Maslow, A. H. (Ed.), *New Knowledge in Human Values*, Harpers. (Included in No. 86). Reprinted in Ard, B. J., Jr. (Ed.), *Counseling & Psychotherapy: Classics on Theories & Issues*, Science & Behavior Books, 1966.

70. Editor, *New Knowledge in Human Values*, Harpers. Hebrew translation, Daga Books, Tel-Aviv, Israel, 1968. Paperback edition, Regnery, 1970.

71. Creativity in self-actualizing people. In Anderson, H. H. (Ed.), *Creativity & Its Cultivation*, Harpers. (Included in No. 86). Reprinted in *Electro-Mechanical Design*, 1959 (Jan. & Aug.). Reprinted in *General Semantics Bulletin*, 1959, 24 & 25: 45–50. Reprinted in Nelson, L. and B. Psaltis (Eds.), *Fostering Creativity*, S. A. R., 1967.

72. Cognition of being in the peak experiences. *Jour. Genetic Psychol.*, 94: 43–66. (Included in No. 86). Reprinted in *Intern. Jour. Parapsychol.*, 1960, 2: 23–54. Reprinted in Stoodley, B. (Ed.), *Society and Self: A Reader in Social Psychology*, Free Press, 1962. Reprinted in Fullager, W., H. Lewis and C. Cumbee (Eds.), *Readings in Educational Psychology*, 2nd Edition, Crowell, 1964. Reprinted in Hamachek, D. E. (Ed.), *The Self in Growth, Teaching, and Learning*, Prentice-Hall, 1965.

73. Mental health and religion. In *Religion, Science and Mental Health*, Academy of Religion and Mental Health, New York University Press.

74. Critique of self-actualization. I. Some dangers of Being-cognition. *Jour. Individual Psychol.*, 15: 24–32. (Included in No. 86).

125

1960

75. Juvenile delinquency as a value disturbance. (With R. Diaz-Guerrero). In Peatman, J., and E. Hartley (Eds.), *Festschrift for Gardner Murphy*, Harper.

76. Remarks on existentialism and psychology. *Existentialist Inquiries*, 1: 1–5. (Included in No. 86). Reprinted in *Religious Inquiry*, 1960, 28: 4–7. Reprinted in May, Rollo (Ed.), *Existential Psychology*, Random House, 1961. Japanese translation, 1965. Reprinted in Hamachek, D. E. (Ed.), *The Self in Growth, Teaching & Learning*, Prentice-Hall, 1965.

77. Resistance to being rubricized. In Kaplan, B., and S. Wapner, (Eds.), *Perspectives in Psychological Theory*, *Essays in Honor of Heinz Werner*, International Universities Press. (Included in No. 86).

78. Some parallels between the dominance and sexual behavior of monkeys and the fantasies of patients in psychotherapy. (With H. Rand and S. Newman). *Jour. of Nervous and Mental Disease*, 131: 202–212. Reprinted in De Martino, M. (Ed.), *Sexual Behavior and Personality Characteristics*, Citadel Press, 1963. Reprinted in Bennis, W., et al., *Interpersonal Dynamics*, 2nd Edition, Dorsey, 1968.

1961

79. Health as transcendence of the environment. *Jour. Humanistic Psychol.*, 1: 1–7. (Included in No. 86). Reprinted in *Pastoral Psychol.*, 1968, 19: 45–49.

80. Peak-experiences as acute identity experiences. *Amer. Jour. Psychoanalysis*, 21: 254–260. (Included in No. 86). Reprinted in Combs, A. (Ed.), *Personality Theory and Counseling Practice*, Univ. of Florida Press, 1961. Digested in *Digest of Neurology and Psychiatry*, 1961, 439. Reprinted in Gordon, C., and K. Gergen (Eds.), *The Self in Social Interaction*, Wiley, 1968. Vol. I.

81. Eupsychia—The good society. *Jour. Humanistic Psychol.*, 1: 1–11.

82. Are our publications and conventions suitable for the per-

126

sonal sciences? *Amer. Psychologist*, 16: 318–319. (Included in No. 86). Reprinted in WBSI Report No. 8, 1962. Reprinted in *Gen. Semantics Bulletin*, 1962, 28 and 29: 92–93. Reprinted in Hitchcock, A. A. (Ed.), *Guidance and the Utilization of New Educational Media: Report of 1962 Conference*, American Personnel and Guidance Association, Washington, D. C., 1967.

83. Comments on Skinner's attitude to science. *Daedalus*, 90: 572–573.

84. Some frontier problems in mental health. In Combs, A. (Ed.), *Personality Theory and Counseling Practice*, University of Florida Press.

1962

85. Some basic propositions of a growth and self-actualization psychology. In Combs, A. (Ed.), *Perceiving, Behaving, Becoming: A New Focus for Education. 1962 Yearbook of Association for Supervision and Curriculum Development*, Washington, D. C. (Included in No. 86). Reprinted in Stacey, C. and M. DeMartino (Eds.), *Understanding Human Motivation*, Revised Edition, Howard Allen, 1963. Reprinted in Lindzey, G. and L. Hall (Eds.), *Theories of Personality: Primary Sources & Research*, Wiley, 1965. Reprinted in Ard, B. J., Jr. (Ed.), *Counseling and Psychotherapy: Classics on Theories and Issues*, Science and Behavior Books, 1966. Reprinted in Sahakian, William (Ed.), *History of Psychology: A Source Book*, Peacock, 1968.

86. *Toward a Psychology of Being*. Van Nostrand. Second edition, 1968. (Includes papers 60, 62, 63, 69, 71, 72, 74, 76, 77, 79, 80, 82, 85, 93). Preface reprinted in *General Semantics Bulletin*, 1962, 28 & 29: 117–118. Japanese translation, Tokyo, Charles E. Tuttle Co., 1964. (Y. Ueda, Translator).

87. Book review: John Schaar, Escape from Authority. *Humanist*, 22: 34–35.

88. Lessons from the peak-experiences. *Jour. Humanistic Psychol.*, 2: 9–18. Reprinted as *WBSI Report*, No. 6, 1962. Digested in *Digest of Neurology and Psychiatry*, 1962, p.

127

340. Reprinted in *Turning On*, 1963, #2. Reprinted in Farson, R. (Ed.), *Science and Human Affairs*, Science and Behavior Books, Inc., 1965.

89. Notes on Being-Psychology. *Jour. Humanistic Psychol.*, 2: 47–71. Reprinted in *WBSI Report* No. 7, 1962. Reprinted in Ruitenbeek, H. (Ed.), *Varieties of Personality Theory*, Dutton, 1964. Reprinted in Sutich, A. and M. Vich (Eds.), *Readings in Humanistic Psychology*, Free Press, 1969.

90. Was Adler a disciple of Freud? A note. *Jour. Individual Psychol.*, 18: 125.

91. Summary Comments: Symposium on Human Values. Solomon, L. (Ed.), *WBSI Report* No. 17, 41–44. Reprinted in *Jour. Humanistic Psychol.*, *1962*, 2: 110–111.

92. *Summer Notes on Social Psychology of Industry and Management*, Nonlinear Systems, Inc., Del Mar, Calif. (Includes papers Nos. 97, 100, 101, 104). Edited and improved revision published as *Eupsychian Management: A Journal*, Irwin-Dorsey, 1965.

1963

93. The need to know and the fear of knowing. *Jour. General Psychol.*, 68: 111–125. (Included in part in No. 86). Reprinted in Peters, H. J., and M. J. Bathroy (Eds.), *School Counseling: Perspectives and Procedures*. Peacock Publishers, 1968. Reprinted in D. Lester (Ed.), *Explorations in Exploration*, Van Nostrand Reinhold, 1969.

94. The creative attitude. *The Structurist*, 3: 4–10. Reprinted as a separate by *Psychosynthesis Foundation*, 1963. Reprinted in the *Ethical Forum*, 1966, #5. Reprinted in Mooney, R. and T. Razik (Eds.), *Explorations in Creativity*, Harper & Row, 1967.

95. Fusions of facts and values. *Amer. Jour. Psychoanalysis*, 23: 117–131. Reprinted in *The Ethical Forum*, 1966, #5.

96. Criteria for judging needs to be instinctoid. *Proceedings of 1963 International Congress of Psychology*, North-Holland Publishers, Amsterdam, 86–87.

97. Further notes on Being-Psychology. *Jour. Humanistic Psychol.*, 3: 120–135.

98. Notes on innocent cognition. In Schenk-Danzinger, L. and H. Thomas (Eds.), *Gegenwartsprobleme der Entwicklungspsychologie: Festschrift für Charlotte Bühler*, Verlag für Psychologie, Gottingen. Reprinted in *Explorations*, 1964, 1: 2–8.

99. The scientific study of values. *Proceedings 7th Congress of Interamerican Society of Psychology*, Mexico, D.F.

100. Notes on unstructured groups. *Human Relations Training News*, 7: 1–4. (Included in No. 112).

1964

101. The superior person. *Trans-action*, 1: 10–13. (Included in No. 112).

102. *Religions, Values and Peak-experiences*. Ohio State Univ. Press. Chap. 3 reprinted in *The Buzz Sheet*, Dec. 1964. Paperback edition, The Viking Press, 1970.

103. Synergy in the society and in the individual. *Jour. Individual Psychol.*, 20: 153–164. (With L. Gross). Reprinted in *Humanitas*, 1964, 1: 161–172. Reprinted in Marvin Charles Katz, *Sciences of Man and Social Ethics*, Branden Press, 1969.

104. Further notes on the Psychology of Being. *Jour. Humanistic Psychol.*, 4: 45–58.

105. Preface to Japanese translation of *Toward a Psychology of Being*, Seishin-Shobo: Tokyo.

1965

106. Observing & reporting education experiments. *Humanist*, 25: 13.

107. Foreword to Andras Angyal, *Neurosis & Treatment: A Holistic Theory*, Wiley, v–vii.

108. The need for creative people. *Personnel Administration*, 28: 3–5, 21–22.

109. Critique & Discussion. In Money, J. (Ed.), *Sex Research: New Developments.* Holt, Rinehart & Winston, 135–143, 144–146.

110. Humanistic science and transcendent experiences. *Jour. Humanistic Psychol.,* 5: 219–227. (Included in No. 115). Reprinted in *Manas,* July 28, 1965, 18: 1–8. Reprinted in *Challenge,* 1965, 21 & 22. Reprinted in *Amer. Jour. Psychoanalysis,* 1966, 26: 149–155. Reprinted in Torrance, E. P., and W. F. White (Eds.), *Issues and Advances in Educational Psychology,* Peacock, 1969.

111. Criteria for judging needs to be instinctoid. In Jones, M. R. (Ed.), *Human Motivation: A Symposium,* Univ. Nebraska Press, 33–47.

112. *Eupsychian Management: A Journal.* Irwin-Dorsey. (Edited version of #92.) (Includes papers No. 100, 101). Japanese translation, 1967; Tokyo: Charles E. Tuttle Co.

113. Art judgment and the judgment of others: A preliminary study. (With R. Morant). *Jour. Clinical Psychol.,* 21: 389–391.

1966

114. Isomorphic interrelationships between knower and known. In Kepes, G. (Ed.), *Sign, Image, Symbol,* Braziller. Reprinted in Matson, F. W., and A. Montagu (Eds.), *The Human Dialogue: Perspectives on Communication.* Free Press, 1966.

115. *The Psychology of Science: A Reconnaissance.* New York: Harper & Row. (Includes paper No. 110). Paperback edition, Regnery, 1969.

116. Toward a psychology of religious awareness. *Explorations,* 9: 23–41.

117. Comments on Dr. Frankl's paper. *Jour. Humanistic Psychol.,* 6: 107–112. Reprinted in Sutich, A., and M. Vich (Eds.), *Readings in Humanistic Psychology,* Free Press, 1969.

1967

118. Neurosis as a failure of personal growth. *Humanitas,* 3: 153–

169. Reprinted in *Religious Humanism*, 1968, 2: 61–64. Reprinted in Bennis, W., et al. (Eds.), *Interpersonal Dynamics*, 2nd Edition, Dorsey, 1968.

119. Synanon and Eupsychia. *Jour. Humanistic Psychol.*, 7: 28–35. Reprinted in H. Ruitenbeek (Ed.), *Group Therapy Today*, Atherton, 1969.

120. Preface to Japanese translation of *Eupsychian Management*. (Included in No. 128).

121. A Theory of Metamotivation: The biological rooting of the value-life. *Jour. Humanistic Psychol.*, 7: 93–127. Reprinted in *The Humanist*, 1967, 27: 83–84; 127–129. Reprinted in *Psychology Today*, 1968, 2: 38–39; 58–61. Reprinted in Kurtz, P. (Ed.), *Moral Problems in Contemporary Society: Essays in Humanistic Ethics*. Prentice-Hall, 1969. Reprinted in Sutich, A., and M. Vich (Eds.), *Readings in Humanistic Psychology*, Free Press, 1969. Reprinted in *Humanitas*, 1969, 4: 301–343. Reprinted in Chiang, H. M., and A. H. Maslow (Eds.), *The Healthy Personality: Readings*, Van Nostrand Reinhold, 1969. Reprinted in Bobbs-Merrill *Reprint Series in Psychology*, 1970.

122. Dialogue on communication. (With E. M. Drews). In Hitchcock, A. (Ed.), *Guidance and the Utilization of New Educational Media: Report of the 1962 Conference*, American Personnel and Guidance Association, Washington, D. C., 1–47, 63–68.

123. Foreword to Japanese translation of *Motivation and Personality*.

124. Self-actualizing and beyond. In Bugental, J. F. T. (Ed.), *Challenges of Humanistic Psychology*, McGraw-Hill. Reprinted in Hamachek, D. (Ed.), *Human Dynamics in Psychology and Education*, Allyn & Bacon, 1968.

1968

125. Music education and peak-experiences. *Music Educators Jour.*, 54: 72–75; 163–171. Reprinted in *The Arts & Education: A New Beginning in Higher Education*, Twentieth Century Fund, New York, 1969.

126. The farther reaches of human nature. *Jour. Transpersonal*

131

Psychol., 1: 1–9. Reprinted in *Psychological Scene* (South Africa), 1968, 2: 14–16. Reprinted in *Philosophical Research and Analysis*, 1970, 3: 2–5.

127. Human potentialities and the healthy society. In Otto, Herbert (Ed.), *Human Potentialities*, Warren H. Green, Inc., St. Louis, Missouri.

127a. The new science of man. In papers on *The Human Potential* for the Twentieth Century Fund, New York.

128. *Toward a Psychology of Being*, 2nd Edition. Van Nostrand. Italian translation, Rome: Ubaldini Editore, 1970.

129. Conversation with Abraham H. Maslow. *Psychology Today*, 2: 35–37; 54–57.

130. Toward the study of violence. In Ng, Larry (Ed.), *Alternatives to Violence*, Time-Life Books.

131. Some educational implications of the humanistic psychologies. *Harvard Educational Review*, 38: #4, 685–696. Reprinted in *Forum for Correspondence and Contact*, 1969, 2: 43–52. Reprinted in *California Elementary Administrator*, 1969, 32: 23–29. Reprinted in *Reflections*, 1969, 4: 1–13.

132. Goals of humanistic education. *Esalen Papers*.

133. Maslow and Self-actualization (Film). Psychological Films, Santa Ana, California.

134. Some fundamental questions that face the normative social psychologist. *Jour. Humanistic Psychol.*, 8.

134a. Eupsychian Network, mimeographed. (Included in No. 128).

1969

135. Theory Z. *Jour. Transpersonal Psychol.*, 1 (2): 31–47.

136. Various meanings of transcendence. *Jour. Transpersonal Psychol.*, 1: 56–66. Reprinted in *Pastoral Psychol.*, 1968, 19: 188, 45–49.

137. A holistic approach to creativity. In Taylor, C. W. (Ed.), *A Climate for Creativity: Reports of the Seventh National Research Conference on Creativity, University of Utah.*

132

138. *The Healthy Personality: Readings.* (with Hung-Min Chiang). New York: Van Nostrand, Reinhold.

139. Notice biographique et bibliographique. *Revue de Psychologie Appliquee* 18: 167–173.

140. Toward a humanistic biology. *American Psychologist*, 24: 724–735.

141. Humanistic education vs. professional education. *New Directions in Teaching*, 2: 6–8.

1970

142. *Motivation and Personality*, Revised Edition. New York: Harper & Row.

143. Humanistic education vs. professional education. *New Directions in Teaching*, 2: 3–10.

1971

144. *Farther Reaches of Human Nature.* New York: Viking Press. (Esalen Series).

145. *Humanistic Psychology: Interviews with Maslow, Murphy, and Rogers.* Willard B. Frick. Columbus: Charles E. Merrill.

1972

146. *Abraham H. Maslow: A Memorial Volume.* Belmont, Calif.: Brooks/Cole.